W9-BRG-371

The Garlic

in the

Melting Pot

By *(signature)* Lewis M. Elia

Edited by Jacquelyn Wolf Birch

ECC Computer Services, Inc.
Desktop Publishing Division
Niskayuna, NY

Copyright 1999 by Lewis M. Elia
ALL RIGHTS RESERVED

PRINTED IN THE UNITED STATES
OF AMERICA

INTRODUCTION

Photo by Stock Studios

Childhood memories too often go unrecorded and drift off like the morning mist. Lew Elia does not let this happen as he stirs up a mystical blend of his growing up experiences. In a series of vignettes, appropriately entitled "The Garlic in the Melting Pot," he, like a Master Chef presents an ethnic background menu that reflects the unique flavor and values of the Italian-American world of yesterday. The ingredients of this recipe are many–family, religion, school, friends and community. Each of these impact all of us but in varying ways and depending on many factors. Yet like the pasta and sauce of a fine Italian meal, the origin can be different yet each is enjoyable. As Lew comments, "Every culture has a new way of thinking, a different way of looking at things. Every language spawns new ideas, the exchange of which helps each of us grow as we continue to forge the new American character." The childhood memories of the author truly reflect a time of transition from the Depression, to World War II and to the sixties when another period of change would take place. It was a time best captured when Lew says, "All of my heroes were cowboys [But] a new kind of western, the adult western, would emerge. The old cowboy was gone forever. The new cowboy liked women more than horses. Sorry old cowboys, I guess we just outgrew you." Perhaps the new generation has, but then again I can still fondly recall those Saturday afternoons at the Congress theater in Saratoga Springs. It was a time when there were clearly defined good guys and bad guys and we didn't seem unsure about who was who.

Thanks Lew for inviting us to your melting pot table where once again we can share the meal of childhood memories that you so lovingly prepared for us.

J. Michael O'Connell, Mayor
Saratoga Springs, NY

Preface

I have often wondered why the most popular books written about Italian families in America are Mafia related stories. I think the reason for their popularity is the same reason that Dante's *Inferno* is read so much more than Dante's *Paradisio*. It seems that people are always more fascinated with the devils and demons than they are with the angels and saints.

Dante's journey through hell yields many more fascinating and colorful characters than does paradise. The author's description of the three headed devil chewing Judas, Brutus and Cassius makes a far more interesting picture than his description of the vision of God. *The Inferno* has gripped audiences for centuries while the *Paradisio* is read chiefly by scholars.

And so it is with the Italian-American family. This book is not about a mob related family and therefore, the stories are really more appropriate to the vast majority of Italian-American families who are not connected to the mob. It is written to honor all the kind-hearted, honest people whose sacrifices for their families added so much to the fabric that became the American nation. It is a tribute to their strength and the endowment they left for us. In that sense, it is a tribute to all immigrant families who added their unique values to the melting pot. Whatever we become, we owe it to them. This is one of their stories.

Lewis M. Elia
June, 1999

This book of memories is dedicated to my children,

Francis, Kevin and Peter

in the hope that they will benefit from the experiences I
had growing up.

A special thanks to my friends:

Lucy Day who helped me organize my original family
journal.
Sally Madgid who did the first reading.

Three great English teachers:
 Miss Helen Doherty, Saratoga Springs High School; Mr.
John O'Hagan, Albany High School; Fr. Charles Hayes,
OFM, Siena College for the faith they had in me while I
was learning.

My Cyber Friends:
Ciaoannam, Unicorn, Gram, for their comments.
k. who helped me think about writing differently.

My Editor:
Jackie Birch for helping me understand the difference
between observing and feeling.

My "Italian Connection":
Dr. Giovanni Spagnuolo, PhD, Assistant Professor at the
University of Salerno, Italy for his help in my research of
the Cilento Peninsula and the Salerno Province of Italy.

MY FIRST RECOLLECTION - JULY 1936

I was sitting on a blanket which my Mother had used as a liner for the basket attached to the handlebars of her bike. There was a lot less traffic in Saratoga Springs in those days. It was late July and a sparkling blue and cloudless sky made a perfect early afternoon. My Mother peddled very slowly and I could feel the bumps as we rode down West Circular Street toward downtown and the park. We passed now long gone landmarks which remain permanent fixtures in my memory. Mother got off the bike and walked it over the railroad tracks, past the freight house and the old Welsh & Gray Lumber Yard. I don't remember going down the rest of the street but I do recall arriving at the entrance to Congress Park and someone making a fuss over me, saying I looked comfortable riding in the basket.

My Mother tells me I was only six months old then. How could I, at that age, understand English? I clearly did! I remember the woman who remarked about my comfort. I don't remember anything else about that day. Perhaps the ride somehow impressed me. I cannot help comparing my Mother now and how she was then. She is now a spry 87, but her stooped frame and tremoring right hand were years away from the strength that was her youth. Like the old Welsh & Gray Lumber Yard (now the site of a senior citizen's center) whose tower I thought would stand forever, she became the inevitable victim of age.

I remember bits and pieces of the years before I went to school. I spent most of my time in my own yard or in the yard of my maternal Grandmother Scarano. In the tiny fenced-in yard next to our rented duplex, I remember the time my Father built a swingset out of solid wood. There were probably no metal swingsets, like the ones you can purchase today and that's why Dad built mine. It was a marvelous contraption that would rival any modern day store package. Not only did it have a tiny ladder that took you to the top of a slide and swing seats that were nice and wide, but chains were ingeniously connected to the seats in four places to prevent them from tipping. The best part, however, was the old tire occupying one of the swing slots. I remember my anticipation as Dad cut the wood, stained it, and put it together. I watched those pieces of wood, that somehow seemed to transform themselves. Although I can do some carpentry myself, I do not have my Father's gift. He matter-of-factly performed his magic, cutting the wood and fitting it so precisely. If I were to attempt to duplicate the same project today, it would take me five times longer and I still would not create the intricacy my Father built into it with such ease. I still marvel at anyone who can do carpentry.

I also remember Dad modifying our heating system. Central heat was unknown in those days (except for people who could afford to own a house.) We had a hand fed kerosene heater. The tank (really a steel barrel) was kept outside on the porch, and the liquid had to be carried in whenever the heater needed it. Dad drilled a hole in the wall, with a hand powered drill, and ran a flexible copper tube directly from the kerosene barrel to the heater. He installed a shut off valve on the inside and now we could fill the tank without having to go outside. When it worked so well, all the neighbors asked him to modify their systems, and Dad, of course, accommodated them without charge. He was a poor businessman, always giving away his skills. I do not recall many instances of our neighbors ever doing anything for him. It always seemed so one-sided to me; perhaps I just don't remember.

SAINT PETER'S ACADEMY

Kindergarten was a lot of fun. I remember the toys and the nun who was little more than a teenager, but first grade (although in the same room) was more serious. The nun was older; there were no toys to use, and we were now expected to read. Sister was surprised to find out that I could already read. I don't know how or when I learned, but I read the headline announcing "Hitler Invades Poland." That was 1939 and I was only four years old. Even though I could read the entire first grade primer with ease, I was the victim of a backward educational policy forbidding any student to get ahead of other students; I was not allowed to go on. I was forced to read the same primer over and over. I got so familiar with it that I could recite it! As a reward, for outstanding scholarship and for exhibiting the best behavior of any boy in the class, I was given a statue of St. Joseph (the best behaved girl got a statue of the Virgin Mary). The behavior part changed as I grew more creative in later years and less tolerant of being bored!

In September of 1941 I began the second grade and I can recall nothing of it except the infamous December 7th Japanese attack on Pearl Harbor. My Father's short time as a shipfitter in the Brooklyn Navy Yard was long enough to qualify him with a skill essential to the war effort. He was ordered to report to the Brooklyn Navy Yard where he helped assemble several aircraft carrier hulls, and we, of course, moved to Brooklyn, NY for the duration.

FAMILY MEMBERS AND PERSONAL HEROS

Many of my family members are to be admired for their accomplishments without the benefit of a formal education. I only wish that they had recorded their recollections for us. I will try to recall some of what I know about them and hopefully will do them justice.

<u>Elia Family</u>

My paternal grandfather, Costabile Elia, married Raffaella Frontoli. My maternal Grandfather, Antonio Scarano, married Filamena Menento. All were born in a tiny seacoast town of Santa Maria di Castellabate in the province of Salarno, State of Campania, Italy. The tiny village is about 25 miles south of the city of Salarno on the southern end of the gulf of Salarno. When they moved to the USA, they landed in New York City with thousands of others and settled in the part of the Lower East Side known as "Little Italy." Their first apartment was in a house that is still standing, located on the corner of Mott and Mulberry Streets. They had taken their parents, my great-grandparents, with them. I remember only my two great-grandmothers who lived into their 90's.

After my Great Aunt Sarah, (my grandmother Elia's sister) married my Mother's uncle Frank Scarano, she become my great aunt on both sides of the family. She could speak perfect, unaccented English, perfect unaccented Italian and fluent Yiddish. Thirteenth Avenue Jewish merchants often mistook Aunt Sarah as one of their own when she argued over the price of bagels and fish in perfect Yiddish. She would take her hard won bargain out of the deli, go one block over to the Italian import store and engage in the same argument in Italian over pepperoni. After stopping to converse with all the English-speaking people on the way, she would drag me over to her house and feed me. I was like a grandchild to her and I thought she was a marvelous person.

4

I often think of what Aunt Sarah could have become if she had been given the opportunity to acquire an education. With her natural talent for languages, she could have been a foreign language teacher or a UN translator. As an immigrant and a woman, she did not even have the chance to go to high school.

Elia Family Tree

Constabile Elia - Raffaella Frontale
(Sister Sarah)

13 Children

Frank Elia   -   Irene Scarnao

Lewis Elia

Circa 1930

An Elia family portrait taken in Brooklyn, NY. My Father
is on the upper left. A girl, Anna died at age seven of
Spanish influenza. Grandma named the next child, her last,
Anna in the Italian tradition.

Scarano Family

Great Uncle Frank Scarano, (my Grandfather Scarano's brother) the oldest of the Scarano family, was orphaned in Italy. Uncle Frank took over the responsibility of providing for the family. He could read and write Italian and was the first to come to America. He had gone to the eighth grade in Italy and worked with fruits and vegetables. When he arrived in the United States, he worked as a produce manager for a major supermarket chain, eventually becoming an inspector of produce for the New York City branch of the corporation. He owned his own home in Brooklyn, NY and educated his first wife's daughter, Catherine who became a New York City elementary school teacher. My Mother's first cousin, she was the only one of our family in her generation who received a college degree. In the Italian tradition, I referred to her as "Aunt Catherine." I remember Uncle Frank coming home from work every night, smoking an Italian stogie cigar, having a shot of whiskey and reading the Italian newspaper. He always had a dog named Princy. When one died the new dog would aldo be named "Princy." After his first wife died, he married my Great Aunt Sarah who had lost her spouse. At the time she had two boys, Louis and Dominic (who we called Monic) Nazzari.

My great-Grandfathers died before I was born. According to the markers on my maternal great-Grandmother's grave, she was born in Campania, Italy before it became part of the Nation of Italy which happened in 1865. What a pity I was not able to know her story! Her name was Rose Trotta. All I can remember about her is that she seemed like an angel to me with her sweet angelic face framed by glowing white hair. When she died, she was waked in my Grandmother's living room and was the first deceased person I had ever seen. But that's getting ahead of the story. Back to New York City. My Mother and Father were born in the same house on Mott and Mulberry. The Elia's stayed in New York and eventually moved to Brooklyn, which was considered "country" in those days. My Father was one of thirteen children, six boys and seven girls. Some died when they were very young. At this writing only three aunts are still living.

My Grandfather Scarano hated city life. He traveled to Saratoga Springs and got a job working on the Delaware and Hudson Railroad. When the depression hit the country, he was laid off along with thousands of others. He got the idea of driving a taxicab during the racing season. He had already learned enough English, passed his driver's test and turned his automobile into a taxicab. While working on the railroad, he eventually saved $3,000 and purchased his home on West Circular Street which had about 1.5 acres of land. This was a tremendous feat, since $3,000 was a lot of money in those days.

My maternal grandparents had five children; Aunt Katie was the oldest, my mother was second. A redheaded boy, Frank, died in what I think was an influenza epidemic when he was two years old. In his section of the cemetery, there are grave markers of several other babies who died at the same time. From the symptoms my Mother described, it seems that he convulsed from the high fever. We still plant flowers on his grave and I visit him often. In an Italian Catholic family this boy is considered to have died a saint since he died an innocent. He always helps me when I visit his grave and pray for his intercession.

The next boy born was my Uncle Jerry and the last of my Mother's family, my Uncle Frank (given the name of the deceased child; also an Italian custom) was born about a year later. Jerry and Frank became successful barbers in Saratoga Springs. My Uncle Jerry owned the barber shop on Phila Street and was very active in civic affairs.

My Father grew up in Brooklyn (not in the same section I lived in) and he and his brothers were dock workers with their father. When Dad was about 20 years old, he decided to go to the races in Saratoga during his vacation time. When Grandmother Elia heard he was going to Saratoga, she immediately remembered her friends, Filamena and Frank who had come from Italy with them. She instructed Dad to visit with them. Dad of course, wanted to go to Saratoga for a good time. The last thing he wanted to do was visit some elderly people from the old country, however, in those days you did what your mother told you to do. He visited. He met my eighteen year old mother, fell in love and got married two years later. Ironically, they had both been born in the same house on the corner of Mott and Mulberry Streets in New York City but never met before. After their wedding, they first lived in Brooklyn. My Mother came home to her mother's house to have her baby (me), and I was born in Saratoga Springs. 1 was then transported to Brooklyn and baptized in the Church of St. Francis of Assisi. My Mother likes to tell the story of my delivery by Dr. Harrington. My Grandfather tried to pay him the $50 before he could take his gloves off. What did you expect from a man who paid cash for his house and car? He would have his grandchild free and clear!

Dad eventually moved his family to Saratoga Springs, working as a carpenter and finally landing a job in the A&P warehouse and commuted to Albany, NY. We moved to a rented duplex on West Circular Street, about half a block up from my Grandmother's house.

Scarano Family Tree

Constabile Menento - Rosa Trotta

Antonio Scarano   -   Filamena Menento
(Brother Frank)

5 Children

Frank Elia - Irene Scarano

Lewis Elia

Palm Sunday, 1924

Scarano family portrait. My Mother, age 12, is on the left
followed by Grandma, Aunt Katie, Uncle Frank, Grandpa
and Uncle Jerry. This picture was taken several years after
my first Uncle Frank (with the red hair) died in the
influenza epidemic at age two.

10

Life in Brooklyn was certainly different from life in Saratoga Springs. We lived on Chester Avenue in a row house in one of four apartments. The neighborhood was in a small area of Brooklyn separated from the larger grid that made up Borough Park. This smaller grid was roughly bounded by Greenwood Cemetery (Fort Hamilton Parkway) on the west, Sixteenth Street on the east, Fifty-Fourth Street on the north, and Thirty-Sixty Street (which had an elevated train in those days) on the south. Much of Borough Park was populated by Hasidic Jews, a smaller part by Italians and non-Hasidics. There was no rhyme or reason to the streets in this smaller section of Borough Park. The numbered streets ended at Thirty-Sixth Street and the next street, which should have been Thirty-Fifth Street was named Chester Avenue. Thirteenth Avenue became Tahama Street. You could walk to the south end of it in five minutes. If you crossed the street at that point (McDonald Avenue) you were in the small area of Kensington and then the larger area of Flatbush where the number grid began again. If you walked a little further that way, you arrived at Prospect Park. I was not allowed to cross McDonald Avenue.

Although this section had no name, it was quite distinct and separate from the rest of Borough Park. Not only did it have definite geographic boundaries, (a natural separation made by the cemetery, the Thirty-Sixth Street EL, the street bordering Flatbush which carried the trolley car line, and Sixteenth Street which was an industrial zone) but it was culturally distinct as well. Jews who were not Hasidic (many of them openly expressed their feeling that the Hasidic were somewhat crazy) and English-speaking, mostly bilingual Italians populated the neighborhood.

The biggest change between Saratoga Springs and Brooklyn was probably the educational system. Communication was not what it is now. Even radio, the only instant mass media of that time, was still young. The resources available to city youngsters were simply not available in a small town. Travel was more difficult. The fastest way to get to Saratoga Springs was a long, five hour train ride. The ride was long because of the number of stops the train had to make. Driving was up Route 9 and took so long it was necessary to stop in Red Hook to eat. When we studied animals in New York City, our class went to the Prospect Park or the Bronx Zoo to see them and talk to the people who cared for them. We were able to go to the Museum of Natural History and attend a lecture by people famous in their field or to Gilbert Hall of Science to see the latest in technological advances.

During the holiday season we went to the Radio City Music Hall, saw a world premier movie being released and a live show. I don't remember the exact year, but the movie at Radio City was the world premier of "Snow White and the Seven Dwarfs." The music hall management had hired real dwarfs to sit atop the marque, dressed as the movie characters, and instructed them to wave to the kids waiting on line to buy tickets. It was a very long line and the wait was about forty minutes. I remember my parents and I waving at the dwarfs. "Hello, you little bastards," one said while another scooped up some snow and threw it at the crowd. Dad found this amusing, my Mother did not. Luckily, we had already passed the marque and were going in the theater at that time. The next day, the morning newspaper carried a story about the incident. Apparently, the dwarfs had been on the marque for some time and decided to warm up by passing around a hip-flask. We had just missed seeing the management pulling the dwarfs back into the theater. The newspaper didn't. Photographers were there photographing the crowd and several pictures of the dwarfs, along with quotes of some phrases they used were featured in the morning paper. This was something no country kid would ever experience, and this was certainly not something you would see in Saratoga Springs.

You would also not see an educational system like New York City schools in Saratoga Springs. A big city school was another world compared to what I had experienced. It was different for me not to be the smartest kid in the class. Education was more progressive and there was no policy of being held back. I loved to read and write stories; at this I was still the best. They forced me to learn mathematics and I did so only to get it over with so that I could go back to writing stories and reading poetry.

Most New York City public elementary school teachers in those days, at least in Borough Park, were Jewish women. I believe that mine was prejudiced against me. I could write better than most kids, but this was not supposed to happen. She buried most of my best stuff in an attempt to avoid embarrassing the rest of the class. I never forgave my teacher for this. At first I thought it was the fact that Italy was an enemy and feelings were running high during the war years with Jews being slaughtered in Europe. Italians were looked upon with suspicion, even though most did not take the least bit of interest in Italian politics, however, I really don't believe that this was the source of her prejudice. Most of the non-Jewish kids in that neighborhood went to Catholic schools, not the public school. Most of the non-Hasidic Jewish kids went to the neighborhood public school. I was one of the few non-Jewish kids to attend this school. It is my belief that my teacher felt I didn't belong there. She thought the school belonged to the Jewish kids who dominated that neighborhood and resented anyone else even living there. I must say, for fear of being misinterpreted, that she was the only one I met in that school who felt that way (or at least showed it.)

Italians in America, and Italian Americans were intensely loyal to this country. The freedom and economic benefits they found here did not exist in pre-war Italy. There were some people, however, who tried to get Mussolini's message over in the neighborhood. One guy would play a phonograph record of Mussolini's speeches from the Fascist

Party. Basically, it was a call for all Italian-Americans to return to the "Old Country" and fight in the Italian Army to restore the Roman Empire. Most of the Italian people in the neighborhood would never consider going back to Italy to fight or for anything else. Some threatened the man's life. He finally disappeared. I don't know if this was the doing of the neighborhood people or the government.

I remember talking with Aunt Sarah, Uncle Frank, and my Grandmother Elia about Mussolini. They agreed that pre-war Italy was pretty bad off economically. They all felt that Mussolini, especially his land reform policy, did a great deal for Italy. They did not agree with the Italian Government's position in siding with Germany. There was a great mistrust of Germans (I Tedeschi.) This was strange since I was quite sure that none of them had ever met a German other than in the United States. They did, of course, remember the First World War and had lost many relatives in the fighting. I personally did not know many German-Americans, but I do remember a rally of the American Nazi Party being held in Times Square and drawing about two thousand people!

KIDS HELP IN THE WAR EFFORT

The war effort had kids doing all sorts of things. We saved the foil from gum wrappers, collected all kinds of scrap metal and bought savings stamps in school. Fill up a book of stamps and you got a war bond! Motion pictures were full of war propaganda. Bowery Boys Leo Gorcy and Huntz Hall were pictured as joining the navy and marines at the end of the movie to do their part (neither of the actors actually served).

Many items were scarce and subject to rationing. Gasoline, butter, and sugar were the most difficult things to get. The government encouraged everyone to grow as many vegetables as they could for their own consumption. These were called "victory" gardens. There was no problem getting

Italians to grow gardens; they could produce a garden on the smallest piece of land imaginable.

New York City was a real blackout community. We learned later that the Germans had flown reconnaissance missions over the city using sea planes launched from submarines. We had frequent air raids in which we had to turn off all lights or pull thick, dark "black out" curtains over the windows. Headlights of cars had to be covered over with only small rectangles cut into the middle of the covers so that other cars could see them. Powerful searchlights from Fort Hamilton and Floyd Bennett Field would search the skies during the blackouts. Many times I saw various aircraft practicing dogfighting over the Brooklyn skies, after taking off from Floyd Bennett Field. I once saw a P-38 (an advanced aircraft in those days) make a fake bombing run in a dive that must have brought it to about 500 miles per hour.

Circa 1928

My maternal Great Grandfather and Grandmother, Constabile and Rosa Manento in the backyard of their home on Elm Street in Saratoga Springs. The yard was filled with fruit trees and grapevines common to the west side Italian community.

VACATIONS IN SARATOGA SPRINGS

I spent each summer vacation with my Grandmother Scarano in Saratoga Springs. These were the happiest days in my life. My cousin Pat, almost two years older than me, and I would go "hunting". We were not allowed to have guns but we pretended to hunt. We saw mostly rabbits, and sometimes a partridge, which we usually scared into flight by accident. Occasionally, we would see a porcupine, a woodchuck and a skunk. We spent a lot of time swimming in the "old water hole" which we called "south bend" near Grand Avenue in Saratoga. A woman writer owned the house and all the land which contained south bend. She never bothered the kids who came there to play. Today, afraid of being sued, she would probably fence it in. We used to go swimming there, (all boys, of course) "bare ass," climb a tree, hang out over the water, hold on to the "family jewels," and jump in from about 15 feet high. It was great fun! If anyone showed fear, he was not a man. I was the best swimmer and diver in the group. The jumping was easy for me even though I was the youngest and the smallest person there.

During the Thanksgiving vacation, we would usually visit my Grandmother Scarano again. The weekend after Thanksgiving was usually "down leaf" time in Saratoga. I remember walking in back of my Grandmother's house with Pat down a dirt path which followed the Delaware and Hudson Line. Their roundhouse was on the left and old Mr. Shinike's farm was on the right. You could peek through the fence of the roundhouse and see the steam engines on the turntable. The D&H tracks continued on the left and miles of open fields would be on the other side, past Mr. Shinike's farm. By that weekend a killing frost had already turned the tall grass and weeds brown and a sort of haze would hang over the fields and the hills in the distance. The dried-up brown leaves would crackle under our feet as we walked down the path and we would occasionally scare a jack-rabbit which would dart out from the grass running in a zig-zag pattern. I often wondered how a hunter could ever have time to raise his firearm, aim and shoot a rabbit. They darted out so fast I could hardly see them, no less aim and fire at one accurately.

Pat was old enough to have a BB gun and he was carrying it with him. After we traveled down the path about a half mile, we would stop and walk into the open field on the right side. In the background was Dilly Lynch's Hill, a sandbank used as construction fill, about a half mile away. No one ever seemed to know who Dilly Lynch actually was. All I knew was that everyone said that was his hill. This was a favorite spot for target practice with the BB gun. We shot mostly at tin cans which had already been poc-marked by countless BB's hitting them during previous practice sessions. Pat and I would take turns firing at the cans. I was not too bad for a city kid but I could not hit as many as Pat did. It was wonderful. I loved the smell of the crisp, cold, autumn air and the feel of the cold metal against my hands and cheek. I loved the brown meadows under the clear blue autumn sky absent of all man-made things. No kid growing up in the city could ever experience this. I thought those fields would always be there when I came home. I was wrong. As the city of Saratoga Springs grew, the hills in the distance would be razed to make way for a new high school. Eventually Mr. Shiniki would die and his farm, along with the adjacent fields and meadows would give way to a housing development. Even the D&H railroad would move its tracks several miles out of town. It's too bad. It was a nice place.

GRANDMA SCARANO; A WOMAN AHEAD OF HER TIME

My Grandmother was a marvel. I believe that I inherited my business skills from her. Unable to read or write in English or Italian, she nevertheless ran a successful business. She developed a wonderful system of bookkeeping and tracking customers. During the racing season, she rented rooms to borders. They shared the refrigerator for food storage. If it had one rubber band around the neck, the milk bottle was ours. Two, and it was the borders in the upstairs front, three the ones in back. During the winter months and times other than the racing season, she took in laundry. Her shed (she called it "shendy,") in back of the house was filled with her customers' crocheted tablecloths and covers that were stretched out on racks with pins placed around the perimeters to simplify drying. Next to each rack was a drawn symbol indicating ownership and a number showing the amount each person owed. Anyone of us could service any customer if we had to. One thing Grandma always knew was how much money anyone owed her.

Grandma was the original conserver of energy. When I was very young, she used wood burning stoves to cook and heat the house. A huge pile of wood would be delivered to the side yard. Pat and I had the job of getting the wood into the cellar. Pat was older and bigger than me so I was ordered to go down into the cellar and stack the wood as he threw it down. Naturally, he had the easier job until my Father checked on us and made us change places.

We also had the job of changing the drip pan in the ice box. A man would come with a horse and wagon loaded with huge blocks of ice, stored under sawdust which would keep them from melting. He would carry them over his shoulder and into the house with a huge pair of black, iron tongs. . As the ice in the ice box melted, the water drained into a "drip pan" located under the box. We would hear, "Pasquale e Luigi, empty the izza-box." Pat and I would take the pan out, which I am sure was kept from overflowing by surface tension. This was careful work, and God forbid you dropped any water on my Grandmother's floor! Out of curiosity, I asked the ice man where he got the ice. He said he cut it out of the pond in the winter and stored it in his barn (under sawdust) where it lasted all summer.

Eventually, Grandma got an electric refrigerator and changed to heating and cooking with coal. She could never master the word refrigerator, which became "refrig" or sometimes "refrig-er-a." All I know is that Pat and I were relieved of drip pan duty. Grandma cooked on a coal-burning stove until coal was no longer available and then she moved to gas. She kept the "ice box" until the man with the horse and wagon died. The upstairs rooms were closed during the winter except for one bedroom where I stayed when I came during winter vacations. She kept it so cold, I don't know how I survived the nights. She had the only six watt bulb I ever saw lighting the staircase to the upstairs. She made the move from wood to coal when she figured it was cheaper because the coal burned longer. Coal was still available when she finally switched to oil. I believed oil was one of the few luxuries she allowed herself because she was getting too old to bank the coal fires at 5 am. Her house had a large grate in the middle of the floor which brought the heat up into the house. Pat, his sister Louise and I would fight to stand on it when we came in from the cold in order to feel the warm air creeping up our pantlegs.

For all her cleverness and business sense, my Grandmother was one of the most superstitious people I ever knew. In preparing for the traditional Christmas Eve dinner, she would make several types of pasta and place them on the dining room table to dry. She was totally convinced that if anyone walked by them and called them "polanta" they would actually turn into that substance. Polanta is a corn meal made with Italian seasoning sometimes known as "Italian Grits." How anyone could believe that pasta could turn into corn meal really tested me. I tried to tell her that this could not happen, and offered to demonstrate. I told her that I would call the pasta "polanta" and show her that nothing like this could possibly happen. Thinking that I would actually do this, Grandma began to cry. Until it reached this point, I am not sure I really believed my Grandmother was serious about this. Obviously she was. She insisted that in Italy, some women were witches and could do things like this. Some only had to look at you to give you the "maloick" the "evil eye" and you would carry this curse with you until the priest came and washed it away with holy water. Others had the power of the devil to curse you by clenching their fist, extending the index and little fingers, and pointing it in your direction. This sign represented the "corna" or "horns" of the devil which cursed you with bad luck if the right person gave it to you. When I talked to my Grandma Elia about this, she confirmed exactly what Grandma Scarano said. She even insisted that she knew a woman who was a "Strega" (a witch) who had come over on the boat with them and now lived in New York. What astounded me was the depth to which these old people held their beliefs in these superstitions.

July 26, 1935

Grandma Scarano in her back yard at 112 West Circular Street in Saratoga Springs. This is the way I remember Grandma. Notice the rabbit huts in the background next to the corn and other vegetables. The rabbits provided meat for the holiday meals. I made the mistake of getting friendly with the rabbits only to have them wind up on the holiday dinner table. I refused to eat it, in spite of my family's efforts to convince me that it was chicken.

Circa 1928

Grandfather Scarano posing proudly in front of his taxicab in front of his home on West Circular Street in Saratoga Springs.

St. Peter's Cemetery, Saratoga Springs, NY

Grave of my first Uncle Frank who died of influenza at the age of two.

In back of Uncle Frank's grave are several other infants who died in the influenza epidemic.

Saratoga Springs, 1929

The very dapper gentlemen are my Uncle Armondo
Ginocchi on the left (my Cousin Pat's Father) and my
Grandfather Antonio Scarano on the right. I don't know
what they are drinking, but I would bet it's homemade
wine.

Kadaross Park, Saratoga Lake, August 14, 1932

My Mother and a friend at the beach. Mother must have had a difficult time convincing my Grandfather to let her wear that bathing suit.

December 8, 1934

Mom and Dad's wedding picture. Grandfather Scarano in front , best man Amelio Jordan on the left, my Father's sister, Aunt Lucy, the maid of honor.

SUMMER ENDS

When summer and vacation ended, it was back to Brooklyn. I used to hate to go back. I loved being in my Grandmother's house and being in Saratoga Springs. I would have to get much older to appreciate what living in Brooklyn taught me.

Most of the time, life in that section of Brooklyn was pretty dull. The older kids in the neighborhood were always bullying the younger kids for something or another. That was pretty much a daily occurrence, but just part of being a kid. On rare occasions, we had to face another menace. I want to emphasis that the incidents I am about to describe were very rare, but they did happen. Most days in my area were pretty dull and not much ever happened.

Once in a while getting to school, even when it was only a few blocks away, could be difficult in Brooklyn. Younger kids might have to face tough kids from the Flatbush section. Every so often these bullies would cross McDonald Avenue and terrorize kids going to our school. Few of them were well organized and it was easy to outsmart them. I had a favorite little bakery, a little building standing next to a house. There was a small alley between the bakery and the house which led to a vacant lot. When I was chased, I would go in the alley and use the drainpipe and a "step" (really a depression in the side of the building) to climb to the roof. I got so I could do this very quickly. Once on the roof, I would lie down behind the two foot "wall" which surrounded the rooftop. I could hear the boys going back and forth trying to figure out where I went. Soon they would leave and I could climb down. On occasion, and only if it was absolutely necessary, I had to fight. This was only done if absolutely necessary, since few of the kids in my neighborhood could beat any of the tough kids from Flatbush. I took a few punches but learned to defend myself. Later, I learned I was less likely to be chased if I walked to school with my friends. We found safety in numbers.

Sometimes we had no choice but to fight. If we were caught by some kids who just were out to beat someone up, we learned to defend ourselves. My edge was that everyone underestimated me. I was small but strong for my size. I could not run very fast (I have very wide feet) but I was capable of very quick movements. I studied judo moves that I read in a book and tried one out on the street. I would walk up very close to my opponent, quickly turn my back to him, reach up over my right shoulder, grab him around the neck and pull down with a bending movement. In Judo, the move is known as a shoulder toss. The first time I tried it, I was as surprised as anyone that it actually worked! Being smaller than my opponent and having a lower center of gravity caused me to send him flying through the air to hit the ground. This startled everyone else, and they ran off. I was a good actor. Astonished as I was, I acted as though I had done it hundreds of times. To my surprise, my opponent was even more astonished. He picked himself up, looked around without making eye contact with me and ran off, probably more out of embarrassment than pain. I never saw him again!

I had to use this move several times. As I became more proficient, I learned to pick out the leader of the group and put this move on him. I quickly realized that if you stung the leader, the rest of them did not fool with you. I even made friends with some of the kids who came to beat me up. I hated the ignorant idea that all they respected was force, but it was a fact of life.

A STRANGE SIGHT

On one occasion I saw a very strange sight. While sitting on my "stoop" (front steps of my house) I watched about one hundred little kids walk down my street on the other side. All were carrying sticks of some sort, which looked to me like broken two by fours. They were walking very close together as if in a military formation. The strange part is that they were all younger and smaller than me, which would make them about five or six years old! They did not do anything except walk by. I do not know what they were looking for and no one stopped to say anything. Needless to say, I did not ask. About ten minutes later, about thirty older kids (perhaps twelve or thirteen years old) came by. They were all carrying baseball bats. They stopped. One came over to me and asked if I had seen a gang of little kids go by. I said, "Yes, about ten minutes ago," and pointed down Chester Avenue in the direction in which they had gone. They thanked me and continued to walk down the street until they were out of sight. I have no idea what happened or where they all went. One learned not to inquire into such things.

I have often thought about that incident. I don't remember any members of the younger gang being more than five or six years old. There was no adult or teenager leading them. Who at that age was able to organize such a group? How could a child so young organize so many into an orderly, military style group, get all of them weapons and march them four abreast down Chester Avenue with such precision? If one could organize so well at that age, where is he now. Did he become a captain of industry, or perhaps an army general? Or did he die in a knife fight in some back alley of Brooklyn. Where did all these kids come from? I didn't see one that was from my neighborhood.

A few years later I was reminded of this incident. The place was the back of number one school in Saratoga Springs.

It was summer and I had just finished 6th grade. There was a huge sand pile in back of the playground which was the remnant of a construction project. We were not supposed to play on it so naturally, it became the site of a "king of the hill" game. You could do anything you wanted (except use a weapon) to get to the top of the hill. Once there, you had to keep the others from pushing you off.

There was a little kid (about 2nd grade) on the top. I never thought about why a little kid was at the top of the hill, but I should have. I walked up and pushed him off. All of a sudden, five little kids jumped me. In a coordinated movement, one grabbed my left knee and another my right knee. One grabbed my left arm and another my right. They pulled me down on my stomach and a fifth jumped on my back. It was impossible to move. They finally let me up, but only when I stopped struggling. I was so shocked, I got off the hill in a hurry. I looked back and saw them do the same thing to another older boy who foolishly thought he could take my place. These little kids had learned the value of teamwork. They made one of their own king of the hill. No one challenged him again.

There were other exiting things about living in a big city. In those years, my Father and I would go to Coney Island. It was a short walk to the West End Subway which connected Brooklyn with Manhattan. For five cents you could go one way and end up in Manhattan, via the bridge (on the express) or the tunnel (on the local.) Go the other way and the last stop was Coney Island (unless, of course you were foolish enough to take the train marked Brighton Beach.) Hundreds of people would pack the subway to Coney Island on Saturday and Sunday. Nothing could match a Coney Island hot dog with everything on it and a bottle of cream soda!

My favorite Coney Island ride was the little car that went though the House of Horrors which featured a replica of every known movie monster and strangely ended with a mannequin replica of Botticelli's "Birth of Venus." I was fascinated by "Venus" who was standing in the altogether, her private parts covered by her long hair, emerging from a giant clamshell with a sea breeze (no doubt caused by a large fan) blowing across her face. In the pre-television days of the 1940's, this was the greatest visual marvel of its day.

Coney Island, Brooklyn, NY June 1937

Dad and I at Coney Island Beech and amusement park, one of the great wonders of the world to kids in those days. Crowds of people would fill the west end subway on weekends for a chance to eat a Coney Island Hot Dog and get away from the city. Kids in Saratoga Springs could only read about Coney Island and were later fascinated to hear that I had actually been there.

Brooklyn, NY 1945

Aunt Sarah (my Grandmother Elia's sister) with her son Monic who had just arrived home after seeing action in the Pacific.

Brooklyn, NY 1945

My Great Uncle Frank Scarano, my Grandfather's older brother who brought up the Scarano Family. His daughter (whom I called Aunt Catherine) is holding Princy. Every dog Uncle Frank had was named Princy.

WORLD WAR TWO ENDS

I remember the end of the war. I was in Saratoga with my Grandmother when the word reached us that we had dropped the atomic bomb on Japan. A few days later, the second bomb was detonated and Japan surrendered . There was absolutely no controversy about using the bomb that I can remember. Everyone was simply glad that the war was over and happy that we had the bomb and not the enemy, for they surely would have used it on us. New Yorkers felt that New York City would have been Germany's first target after London. The propaganda value would have been perfect for the Nazis. We would have been right under it. I personally agree with the decision to drop the bombs. I believe if we had not seen what nuclear weapons were capable of doing, more would have been used by one side or the other at a later date. The widespread destruction of the blast along with the radiation fallout was so horrible that no one would dare risk it again. That was the attitude in the years of the cold war that followed. You will have to make up your own mind about it, but remember, more Japanese died in the firebombing of Tokyo than did under the atomic bomb. General Curtis LeMay ordered low level incendiary bombing of Tokyo knowing that the Japanese housing were made of wood and paper. In addition to the people who died from direct hits and from the accompanying fire, thousands more died from asphyxiation caused by the extremely hot fires using the oxygen supply. This type of bombing killed even the people who were in bomb shelters.   Why not the controversy there? It was almost as if the firebombing was an expected thing in a war. It required many more planes and supplies to make that raid, only one plane to drop the A-bomb. Although thousands more died in conventional and fire bombing, it did not present the same horror that was caused by the blast and radiation from an atomic weapon.

BACK TO SARATOGA SPRINGS

Everyone was happy that the war was finally over. I was very happy that we were finally going to move back to Saratoga Springs, but not prepared to face the new trials that I was about to endure. I began my next grade in No. One School in September of 1945. What I did not expect was the provincial attitude of the children of Saratoga. Different from the cosmopolitan big city kids, the small town kids had not been exposed to different kinds of people, ideas, cultures, life styles, etc. that I had witnessed. They seemed very ignorant to me. Despite the variety of people summertime in Saratoga brought, they still did not lose their provincial attitudes.

I remember remarking in class that I had witnessed many people in New York City who could speak other languages. This prompted one of my classmates to ask how it was possible for anyone to speak another language if they could not speak English first. This in turn prompted my teacher to launch upon a lengthy explanation about other native tongues. I sat disbelieving that anyone had to have this explained to them.

I was surprised to find myself being taunted by kids on my way to school. Everyone had heard of the kid from New York and some wanted to see how tough I was! At first I tried to ignore them. If my cousin Pat was with me, they left me alone, but he was sometimes with his friends. Besides, he told me "Kick somebody's ass and they will leave you alone." There was one kid, (I will call him Joey,) who would not let it go. He was not a particularly tough kid, and I was able to push him away. He charged at me and knocked me down. He gloated over me, not knowing that I was feigning injury. I got up slowly, walked up next to him, turned my back, grabbed his neck and threw him in the air. He broke his arm when he landed. My old trick worked again but with much better results. The Principal, a woman, scolded me for being so violent. I explained that I had been trying to avoid fighting with Joey but could not. My Father came and apologized to the Principal; he told me later that I had no choice but to defend myself, the arm thing was an accident. Dad said it didn't cost anything to apologize but told me to go on defending myself. He also told me never to start a fight. I was never bothered again. Joey wanted to become my friend. It sickened me to think that the only thing he respected was force.

Later, as I reflected on this incident, I realized that Dad was still clinging to the "us and them" philosophy of the immigrant family. Even though he was born in this country, he had a mistrust of people in positions of authority. You put on one face for them and another for life in the streets. It did not occur to me at the time, but I don't remember Joey being called in the Principal's office and being scolded for being so violent.

A DIFFERENT SIDE OF THE SMALL TOWN

At the end of grade six, we moved to an apartment on Broadway. This meant a change of schools from school one to school three. School three was totally different, populated by poor kids from Saratoga's north side, almost all Angle-Saxons. Kids with names like Pratt and King and a few Irish and German ones were my new classmates.

The first day, a couple of kids chased me, but I had learned how to handle being chased back in Brooklyn. Almost everyone was faster than I was, so I developed a trick to cope. I would run as fast as I could. My opponent would chase and almost catch me. When I was just within his grasp, I'd stop and fall down on all fours. Caught by surprise and unable to stop at that high speed, my pursuer would trip over me, falling on his face. I would then spring up, jump on him, and land my two feet in the middle of his back. This would knock the wind out of him and he would be unable to chase me. I had to use this move going to Number Three School. A boy, Tom Bosley, saw this and came to my aid. I still don't know why Tom decided to be my friend, but I was surely glad he did. He was the best athlete in the school; no one fooled with him. Being Tom's friend made everyone else my friend. We played a lot of ball together, winning the sixth and seventh grade elementary championships in baseball, touch football, basketball and soccer. Tom lives in Saratoga today and although we went our separate ways, we still visit once in a while.

Our basketball team was so good, we had to play teams from out of town to get some competition. The school authorities arranged for a Catholic school from a nearby city to come in and play us. We were scared when we saw them. They had real uniforms with numbers and white sneakers. Our kids had nothing that matched and came pretty much in rags and torn sneakers. I wore the only pair of new sneakers. They had a real coach who put them through real warm up drills. We had no coach. We had never seen a real warm-up drill! The game began. I stole the ball from their guard, darted toward the basket and missed. Tom followed up and made the shot! We kicked their ass all over the court. They were absolutely no match for us; they simply and only *looked* better! (The difference between substance and form ?).

A BOOK AND ITS COVER

There were not many African-Americans living in Saratoga Springs in those days. Most just came in during the racing season to work. Near my Grandmother's house, there was one older lady who lived by herself. You had to walk down an alley to get to her small house (a converted garage?). She kept pretty much to herself. All the kids in the neighborhood said she was some kind of strange woman. I remember being terrified of her. One day my Grandmother gave me a package instructing me to take it to her. I was petrified, but dared not refuse. I was sure the black woman was going to cook me in the oven or something. With my knees shaking, I went down the alley and knocked on her door. She answered; I handed her the bag. She said she had something for me to bring back and invited me inside. I went in and stood just inside the door. At the first sign of trouble, I was ready to make a break. I could be at my Grandmother's house before anyone could catch me! The woman came out of her kitchen with cookies and milk that I could have while she was getting my Grandmother's package together. Some voodoo lady! She was the nicest woman you could ever meet and I learned a great lesson that day. I would be more careful about forming judgments of people based upon what others perceived.

TOOLS AND ENCYCLOPEDIAS

My birthday was coming up and my Father and I discussed my gift choice. He suggested a set of tools so that he could teach me carpentry. I told him that I preferred a set of encyclopedias and an atlas. He could not understand my preference for books over a perfectly good set of tools. Tools would be with me for the rest of my life and could even help me make a living. What could you do with these books? What good was a book with a map of Switzerland? Dad gave in; I got the books but he never could understand my choice. I know that during his two years in high school in Brooklyn his instructor wanted him to become an architect. Dad wanted to become a carpenter. Although he could have done architecture, it was probably an unrealistic choice for him. Dad liked to be on the working end of things and could never relegate himself to drawing plans in an office. This was reflected in his attitude about the books verses tools. His concern was for my future. How could I ever make a living without any skills or a trade?

IS CORN SILK GOOD TO SMOKE?

According to my cousin Pat and the rest of the kids in the neighborhood, corn silk was good to smoke. My Grandmother had plenty of corn growing in her garden and by late summer the sun had cured the silk. You could put it in a corn-cob pipe, light up, and smoke it like it was real tobacco. Of course I wanted to try it because everyone else was smoking. It made me kind of sick, but I would never let on to the rest of the kids and especially not to my cousin Pat (although he was probably feeling the same thing). Right in the middle of a drag, my Father walked out from the cornfield. We were caught!

Now you must understand my Father. He had his way of doing things. He never used corporal punishment; his method was more permanent. I will never forget the beautiful act he put on. He had Pat and me convinced that he was very hurt by the fact that we were smoking behind his back. If we were going to smoke, it would be far better to be open about it. He, in fact, would buy us our first cigar! Pat and I could not believe it. We made some reference to our Mothers not approving, but Dad said he would explain it to them. After all, we were men and should be able to smoke if we wished (I was about eleven and Pat was about twelve and a half). He produced an Italian Stogie and cut it in half deciding to smoke with us. We lit up, took a drag, and I was unable to take another. When I looked at Pat, he had already turned green. We spent the rest of the afternoon vomiting. I could not eat right for about three days. My Mother and my Aunt Katie were certainly in need of explanation. Although they were plenty mad at my Father, they should not have been. All through high school Pat and I were never again tempted to smoke. To this day, I cannot figure out how anyone can smoke an Italian Stogie!

Every September in Saratoga Springs, the Italian neighborhood used to have a festa in honor of St. Michael whose feast day occurred in that month. When I was very young, the feast was a Saratoga event. The square on Beekman Street was closed to traffic and a bandstand was built. During the day, a greased pig was let loose and every kid in the neighborhood tried to catch it and win a prize. A fifteen foot pole was erected and greased and a wooden circle was built on the top from which hung a bottle of Chianti, a huge salami, a mozzarella cheese, a handful of dollar bills and various other objects. Anyone who could get to the top could keep the prizes he could bring down. Teenagers drew lots to determine their position and all tried to climb the pole. It was best to be about fifth or sixth in line so the first climbers would wear the grease off the pole. Usually the fifth or sixth climber would make it to the top and attain victory.

After we consumed all the cotton candy and pizza friete we could handle, night fell and the band would play. People would dance in the streets and once in a while, a few fireworks would be thrown up to liven up the party. At nine o'clock, it was time to go south of town to Globenson's Corners where the big fireworks display would take place. Cars would jockey for the best spots and families would put blankets down on the ground for good seating at the big show.

For kids, the highlight of the show was the aerial bomb which contained the parachute flare. After the aerial burst a little parachute, imbedded in the bomb, would open carrying a very bright, white flare lighting up the entire countryside. The chute would open at a great height and float to ground, usually about a half mile away. It seemed that every kid in Saratoga was chasing the flare which went out before it ever hit the ground. This meant that the chute could no longer be seen and everyone had to figure out where it was going to land by using nothing but dead reckoning. Sometimes the chute was not found until the next day. The fireworks always ended with a ground display which featured the Italian and American flag displayed in red, white and blue flares. Displaying the American flag was a good way to get the crowd to stand up and cheer and a good way to end the festa.

When I was about twelve years old, the feast was beginning to lose the support it once enjoyed. The event was sponsored by the Princess Elena Society, a local men's social club, whose members were ageing and whose numbers were declining. Consequently, the feast was beginning to get smaller every year. Most of these older men were born in Italy and could not interest younger Italian-Americans in joining the organization. The old neighborhood was beginning to change as the younger men and women were moving into the mainstream of American life. Following the American dream of the house in the suburbs, the two and one-half children and the big back yard, few, if any, were willing to invest in the old neighborhood and bring up their families there.

For some of the old men, hope sprung eternal. I remember the opening speech, made by the chairman of the festa committee. Wearing his best suit, which rarely saw the light of day, and a hat which looked like it just came out of the box, he addressed the small crowd from the newly finished bandstand.

"Ladies and-a-gentlemen," he opened. " This-a-year, we-a-gonna have-a bigger and-a-better celebration-a then-a last-a year." We gonna have-a more lights-a, more booths-a, more firework-a then-a last-a year."

The festa got smaller and smaller every year. The old man made the same speech every September until he died.

RELIGIOUS INSTRUCTION

A large part of growing up in an Italian Catholic family involves the religious instructions we were required to master. In the 1940's, the religious education programs was mostly taught by nuns who were regular teachers in the Catholic schools. They reflected attitudes that pre-dated Pope John XXIII and the Vatican II reforms. Many parishes were still "national" churches reflecting the makeup of the various neighborhoods which were mostly ethnic in nature and just beginning to emerge from using their native tongues.

In Brooklyn, NY the churches of St. Francis of Assisi and St. Catherine of Alexandria were overwhelmingly Italian. Some masses, although still said in Latin, had sermons spoken in Italian. Many of the sisters, as well as the priests, were either from Italy or Italian-American. Being an elementary school pupil, I received basic catechism which centered on such questions as "Who made you?" "God made me," was the proper answer. We also had to learn the "Hail Mary," "Our Father." and the "Act of Contrition," by heart. If we were unable to recite any of those prayers perfectly, we risked eternal damnation and eternal suffering according to our teachers. Since hell did not sound like a place where I would even like to visit, I was motivated to master these prayers quickly. Eventually, I made my First Communion at St. Catherine of Alexandria in Brooklyn. Shortly thereafter, my family would move to Saratoga Springs and I would begin my preparation for Confirmation in Saratoga Springs at my old parish, the Church of St. Peter.

St. Peter's parish in Saratoga Springs had originally been an Irish National Church. When American parishes were formed in the United States they were usually formed along the lines of national origins. It was thought that this would be easier for Catholic immigrants who could hear sermons in their own language and make an easier transition for the people and the church in America. Unlike Protestant churches which were organized along denominational lines, Catholics did not have denominations expressing different dogmas. Most Protestant denominations in America originated in the British Isles and spoke English, so the problem was not as acute for them. Among Roman Catholics, the Irish were the only English speaking group. Where I was growing up, Italians and Poles were forming their parishes along ethnic lines. Eventually these groups mastered the English language and blending into the English speaking society. Even after they achieved this, national churches persisted; traditions die hard. Since there were not enough Italians in Saratoga Springs to form an Italian National Church, we had to take our religious instructions in a church that was originally formed by Irish Catholics from the Diocese of Albany. Some of the nuns were imported from Ireland. My Religious Instruction program was now at a higher grade level. At this grade level the instruction dealt with more advanced topics. The pre-Vatican II Catholic attitude of those days became more apparent to me as the sisters of St. Joseph (the teaching order at St. Peter's Academy) tried to explain Catholic theology and guide us into a holy adult life.

It is obvious to me now that all nuns in those days were not very well versed. This was probably true of the Brooklyn sisters as well as the sisters in Saratoga Springs, but in Brooklyn we had not gotten far beyond "Who made you?" Some of the Saratoga nuns had some rather strange notions about Christianity. I vividly recall one stating that it was not required of Catholics to believe in angels. She went on to back her reasoning with the fact that angels were not mentioned in the Apostle's Creed, and we only had to believe in what was stated in the Creed. My reaction to this was, "Who was singing on Christmas Night, the Episcopal Choir?" Of course I got in trouble for this. I was, after all, only a kid and still afraid of eternal damnation so it was easy to squash my interpretation of Catholic theology. The sisters were effective in their ability to keep me quiet but were not able to change my thoughts. If I had accepted this sister's interpretation of Catholicism, a great deal of the New Testament turned into mythology. Giving up my belief in angels meant that the angel Gabriel never appeared to the Virgin Mary and stated "Hail Mary full of grace, the Lord is with thee," as I had so patiently committed to memory. Many other things in the bible would have had to change as well. Even worse, the annual Feast of St. Michael the Archangel, sponsored by the Italian Community of Saratoga Springs could be canceled along with the fireworks!

It was not unusual for all teachers in those days to promote strange practices. Public school teachers were no exception. Most public school teachers were products of "normal" schools, designed by the state to assure the public a supply of teachers and had not had much more preparation then my religious instructors. These schools kept the state from experiencing a teacher shortage but did not necessarily produce well informed teachers. I recall my public school teacher in Brooklyn insisting that when we spelled a word containing a double letter aloud in front of the class, we had to pronounce it "double s" or "double t" as the case may be. Therefore, if asked to spell the word "appear," they *had* to say "a-(double p)-e-a-r," and not "a-p-p-e-a-r. We had misspelled the word if we did not say "double p." Of course everyone did what the teacher said, but as I grew older and thought about it, I often wished I could go back and ask that teacher to spell the word "vacuum."

In New York City, which should have had the most advanced school system in the world, teachers with silly notions and methods could fashion a career. I can only conclude that teaching in those days was not on a par with the profession as it exists today. The idea of keeping educational costs down took precedence over quality in education.

Teaching, especially in the elementary schools, was looked upon as a woman's job. Requirements to earn a lifetime teaching certificate for elementary schools were not heavy and the public got what it paid for. Part of the reason the incompetence persisted and was tolerated is that parents of working class people felt uncomfortable talking to the educated. They were not equipped with the verbal skills and did not see education as necessary anyway. You could make a living as a barber, carpenter, tailor or in construction but what the heck could you do with book learning anyway?

Getting back to religious instruction, our Saratoga nun also coached us on how to take communion. According to her, it was very important that the Body of Christ not be chewed. One should take the host in the mouth, make very sure it did not touch the teeth, place it on the back of the tongue, allow it to dissolve and swallow it. I was very careful to do this, of course, not wanting to be responsible for chewing the Body of Christ which had already suffered enough. Soon after school was out, we were visiting family in Brooklyn and decided to go the St. Francis of Assisi Church for mass. That Sunday, the communion was distributed in a basket and in place of a wafer, the bread was in the shape of little loaves. They were slightly larger than a bite size cereal and had a very hard crust. It was *impossible* to swallow it without chewing it. I kept it in my mouth for a long time pondering what I would do to Our Lord if I sunk my teeth into it. When I looked around me and saw everyone else chewing, I decide to chew it also. If I had to go to hell for this, so would everybody else!

Back in Saratoga Springs, the time for Confirmation was about to arrive. Stories were circulating about the Bishop slapping everyone in the face, an action which enlisted you in the Army of Christianity for the rest of your life. This could not have been as bad as having to sit quietly in the pews of St. Peter's Church for over an hour a day listening to the priest's instructions on the awesome duties of becoming a soldier of The Church. The pews in St. Peter's were slightly unusual in the fact that the wooden backs had a convex curve starting at the base of the spine which put an unmistakable impression in the small of your back. I can assure you that no mediaeval monk, however much engaged in self-immolation, ever had to sit in one of St. Peter's pews for over an hour a day.

When the big day came and the Bishop finally arrived, all students were on their best behavior. We had about two hundred young people being confirmed, and the church was filled with them and their sponsors. It was interesting to look at the sponsors. Many of them had not been in church for years. It would have been a perfect place for the FBI, since every bookie in town had been chosen as someone's Confirmation sponsor. The demand for bookies as conformation sponsors was high and only the lucky kids got them. These were only boys, since there were no women bookies. The best a girl could do was to have the wife of a bookie as a confirmation sponsor. That assured you of the same things the boys received, which was riding to the event in a big car and receiving a large monetary gift at your party. We went to the altar in single file, each sponsor placed his or her hand on the shoulder of the confirmee and His Excellency slapped the Holy Spirit into each soul and enlisted us into the eternal service of the church.

When I got home, I experienced the rewards of being confirmed. My Confirmation party at my Grandmother's house rivaled the one my cousin Pat had two years earlier. The food was spectacular. Italian families traditionally give money to each other at these events. Communions, confirmations, weddings (especially weddings) usually bring a shower of monetary gifts which the person is expected to remember and return in kind when the time comes. Italian families tend to be very close and supportive of one another. Food and money are high on the list as the way to articulate

A TOWN THAT LIVED ON GAMBLING

Saratoga Springs was a town that lived on gambling. It does to some extent today, being the site of America's oldest, active racetrack. But for all the racing tradition, the Saratoga of the late 1940's was still a wide open gambling town. During the month of August, one could find any kind of action. Roulette, craps, blackjack, poker, etc., flourished in the Saratoga night clubs. If you made money at the track, you could lose it all at the roulette wheel or crap tables that night. Full fledged gambling casinos could be found which featured big time acts of the day like Joe E. Lewis and Sophie Tucker. This type of gambling was not legal. Only horse racing was legal, but no one seemed to care. The population of the town would rise from sixteen thousand to over fifty thousand during the month of August.

Employment opportunities abounded for local people who wanted to hustle for a buck. Some local girls became ladies of the evening during the summer months, earning a good enough living to get them through the rest of the winter. I did a variety of jobs which included selling tip sheets to the racing customers. These tip sheets were the picks of local entrepreneurs who were willing to help pick winners in races for a quarter. They were of course, all favorites picked for win, place and show and would always contain a few winners. The best customers we had were old ladies. They were also the only ones who tipped us. Senior citizens with big hearts and a dream of getting rich. Today, the government sells them the same dream with off track betting and the lottery but at much longer odds. I received a nickel for every sheet I sold.

My most interesting job was cleanup and gofer boy in the back room of a store which held poker games. It was a simple concept. The owner would supply the table, along with cards and poker chips in return for a small percentage of each pot. Drinks and cigarettes were extra, but no alcohol was served. My job was to bring cigarettes and drinks to the patrons and help keep the place cleaned up. I got ten dollars a night plus tips. There were about twelve tables in that back room. I could take home about twenty dollars on a good night.

I learned a great deal about the psychology of gambling from the owner. He taught me to be very observant and make a mental note of who was winning. When a hand was over, I was to go to that table and make sure I cleaned up any cigarette butts or cans that were near the winner. This increased my chances of receiving a tip, since people who were winning were feeling flushed and were freer with their money. At the same time, I noticed that he was also at the table taking his percentage out of the winner's pot. The psychology at work was a thing of beauty. Everyone thought of this owner as a good guy because he only took money from the winners, never from the losers. They were obviously not smart enough to figure out that it was their money in the pot. The winners were happy to pay since they considered this found money anyway. Such is the psychology of the gambler. He can never win. If he loses, he must keep gambling and try to get even. If he wins, the money comes easy and he either spends it quickly or begins taking greater risks in a vain attempt to gain more. I never saw anyone who actually ended up winning money. If they walked away from the table ahead, they were always broke in one or two days. I noticed that the man who owned the place never gambled. He never played cards or ever bet on a horse. He was the only one I saw who ever made money. My lessons on gambling became clear to me. The only "gamblers" that ever win are the ones who run the game. They never gamble.

THE HORSE WHISPERER?

In Saratoga Springs, before 1950, horseback riding was something a poor kid could enjoy. One only needed to go a short distance out of town on Saratoga's west side to run out of the residential neighborhood and reach the farm lands and woods. About a mile west of my Grandmother's house was a horse farm which had horses for hire. For seventy five cents we could rent the use of a mighty steed and spend the better part of three hours riding through a well established horse trail. This trail passed through a set of beautiful woods and meadows which nobody seemed to own. After about an hour and a half the trail ended at the top of Dilly Lynch's Hill where all the horses in the party were stopped momentarily to rest the horses and give the riders a chance to look down on the west side neighborhoods of Saratoga Springs. Of course, we could see our houses from there. My cousin Pat and I would always spot our Grandmother's little brick residence clearly visible close to the D&H railroad tracks and roundhouse. We could also see Pat's house right across the street from Grandma's. The puffs of white smoke from the steam engines performing their switching duties in the rail yards made the houses and the neighborhood look like a model railroad set. After the horses were rested, we would trace our way back to the horse farm and spend some time talking with the owner.

The owner was a fascinating character named Sheddy Evans. In our minds he knew everything there was to know about horses. He owned a western saddle, an English saddle, a fancy Mexican saddle and several others. On our trips we always used the western saddles, the others seemed to be around more for conversation and an occasional horse show. His horses were all well trained, well behaved animals. Evans did everything but hold a conversation with them and sometimes I wonder if that didn't happen.

These horses definitely knew Evans' touch. He always brushed them down after they had been saddle ridden or after they had pulled the open carriage that he kept in the back of his barn. One could see the love in their eyes when Evans took off their saddles and stroked them on the side of the neck. They would inevitably turn, look at him and blow through their lips like a cat purrs when it is stroked. He spent hours picking burrs out of their manes and brushing them down. After a while, we were allowed to help with these tasks and found out that the animals bonded with us when we took care of them. No one could ever achieve the complete bonding with the horses that Evans was able to, but we did learn that these animals were living, feeling beings that could sense we were being kind to them.

Pat and I loved horseback riding. We did everything we could to save our money so we could go once a week. Evans was very good to us. He taught us how to handle the horse with the feel of our legs. "Get your hands off that saddle horn," he would say when he saw us grip the horn of the western saddle to steady ourselves. "The horn is for tying a rope onto, not for steadying yourself. Get the *feel* of that mare and she'll get the feel of you. Lead the horse right and she'll do anything you ask her to do." Although he never put it in so many words, he taught us that if we were firm and gentle with a horse, we and the horse could become one.

In the years that followed, horseback riding became an upscale sport and poor kids were priced out of it. The economic growth of the fifties was fueling the move to the suburban areas, and a different class of people were discovering the sport. The new money arriving in these rural areas began inflating the prices and horses were no longer available for hire at a price we could afford. The inevitable law of supply and demand was beginning to price us out of the market. Even the old horse trail was disappearing as the owners, realizing the value of the land, began selling out to developers. People were willing to pay more for riding on shorter trails for less time. I don't know what happened to Evans, but I suspect he spent most of his life around horses.

Some of the land that was crossed by horse trails had been developed into golf courses. The economic forces at work here were somewhat different. Golf, which has been dominated by the upper socio-economic class, was now being taken up by a different class of people. The influx of this new class of people was changing the game of golf and was another contributing factor to the disappearance of the old horse trails.

I often thought about what big city kids missed because they could never know horses the way I had known them. If they had seen a real horse, it was probably because their parents took them to the race track. Most of my Brooklyn friends' concepts about horses were conceived from the cowboy movies they sat through on Saturday mornings at the Radio Theater on Thirteenth Avenue. Seeing a horse in a movie could never convey the feel of the real animal. A picture of a horse is not a horse, not in the sense that anyone could get the look, feel and smell of a real horse. Beyond that, they could never feel the *love* of the animal. They could never feel the movement of a horse with their legs. Some thought they had ridden a "horse" at the Steeplechase Ride in Coney Island. They could get strapped to one of the lifeless steel horses which glided along on rails. This was fun, but they could only feel the cold, lifeless black steel when they put their hand on the horse's neck. They could never experience the feel of a warm, wet neck on the real animal and experience the bond between themselves and the living animal that was breathing, snorting and filling the rider's nostrils with the smell of sweat and leather. They could never know the real love of riding.

As horseback riding disappeared into the upper social set, poor kids could only experience a simulated horse by riding the merry-go-round at Kadeross Amusement Park at Saratoga Lake. The merry-go-round was a unique experience in itself. Artistically carved horses gliding on brass poles would go around in circles for what seemed the longest time. The simulated horses were all painted in bright colors, mostly white with blue, red and gold saddles. The brass poles passed through each horse where the saddle horn would have been on a western saddle. The horses were all carved in running positions, some with their heads down as if someone were pulling back on the reins catching the bit in the horse's teeth; others had their heads up as if they were finishing a jump. The ring of horses on the outside of the merry-go-round were stationary; the inside ring of horses went up and down as the carrousel turned. You could strap yourself into an outside, stationary horse and try to catch the brass ring for a free ride or get into the inside ring and have your horse go up and down as you rode. You could also ride in one of the "half-shell" seats. This, of course, was only for adults since no self-respecting kid would ever pass up a ride on a horse to sit in a seat and just go around and around. What kind of fantasy would that have been?

One of the most fascinating things about the merry-go-round was the mechanical band that played during the ride. Crafted before the days of electronics, this marvelous thing would beat a bass and snare drum, clang symbols, toot a horn and play a piano with the precision of a real brass band. I counted at least six merry-go-round type songs before I heard one repeated.

As time passed, the little mechanical band began to break down. Although the tunes were still recognizable, some of the instruments no longer played. There must have been no one around who could fix it, because it was eventually replaced by an electronic tape recorder. Somehow, the tape recorder could never capture the sparkle of the little mechanical band that beat the drums and clanged the symbols. In time the Kadeross Amusement Park was sold to a company that developed it into condominiums. The merry-go-round was dismantled and the structure which housed it was renovated into an exercise club for the residents. The amusement park with its beautiful merry-go-round became a part of Saratoga history.

ALL OF MY HEROES WERE COWBOYS

Children all over America had many major influences that brought them out of their ethnic backgrounds and into the mainstream of American society. The great public school which helped them master the English language; mixing with people from other cultures; sports heroes that everyone knew. These things infiltrated Italian family life and contributed to the making of the Italian-American, however, one of the most underrated influences on all American children was the impact of the American movie cowboy.

The years between 1865 and 1885 saw the end of the Civil War and the expansion of the American west. A free and open spirit and a brand of rugged individualism, coupled with a lack of law enforcement authorities, which prevailed in the western territories of those days gave rise to the term "wild west." The real west and the west written about in the dime novels of the day were vastly different. Many of those stories were really romantic adventures aimed at selling the books to eastern couch potatoes who were eager for escape literature. Much of what was written, no matter how much the incidents they were based upon were true, rarely conformed to the actual facts.

History tells us that the only true "gunfight" that ever took place was when Wild Bill Hickcock shot a man in the heart. Most gunfights were wild affairs and most men were really ambushed and shot in the back. Yet countless stories were told about gunfights between highly skilled warriors most of whom conformed to a code of honor and fought a fair fight. Almost none of it ever happened that way.

Enter the movies, and the romance of the old wild west moved from the dime novel to the silver screen. This new technology would provide a stage where the wild west could come alive to a mass audience. In typical Hollywood fashion, the old stories were re-written and new twists were added. Many more myths about the old west would grow from the movies. One of these had to do with the notion of wagon trains, attacked by bands of Indians. The settlers immediately drove their wagons into a circle, creating a fort as a way to defend themselves. In truth, settlers never did this. The first time it was ever mentioned was when it was depicted in an early western film made about 1933. Motion picture equipment was not very advanced in those days and a method of filming a wagon train under attack had to be found that would not require many movements of the camera equipment. The director came up with the idea to circle the wagons as a way to achieve this. So a technique invented to make filming easier exploded into an icon of the American west and "circle the wagons" became a phrase which to this day is still used to describe defending oneself.

The movie cowboy who evolved during the 1940's really reflected the ideals of the society at that time rather than any real person of the old west. The cowboy hero was always clean shaven and his clothing was always neat and clean. He was very chivalrous and never swore or used vulgar language. The considerable gun fighting skill he possessed was always used to fight the good fight, usually protecting the rights of ladies and hard working families from unscrupulous men who were trying to exploit them. He was unmarried, had a horse that was more intelligent and loyal than most of the people in the film and never seemed to have a job. He had no family of his own, answered to no one and always fought the good fight. He was fiercely independent, had a great singing voice and was as proficient with a guitar as he was with a six-gun. This hero always managed to win a fight even when he was framed, and always moved on after solving the town's problems and getting rid of all their bad guys. He always managed to pick up a "sidekick," whose antics provided the comic relief for the story line. He had all the attributes of a medieval knight with a handgun replacing the lance and sword.

To the 1940's kids, he was a saint. His success as a role model was so universal it crossed ethnic, social, economic and geographic lines. It made no difference who the kids were or where they lived, their heroes were cowboys. Irish, Italian and Jewish kids in Brooklyn attended the movies every Saturday morning to worship these heroes just as Anglo-Saxon kids in Saratoga Springs did. Everyone owned at least a cowboy hat and a set of cap pistols complete with holsters emulating their favorite cowboy. In mock gunfights, we all wanted to be the good cowboy. We had to take turns at who was to be the bad guy and get shot. Sometimes we just got the guns shot out of our hands; other times we aped the actors and played out a long death scene. Bad guys always took a long time to die.

Children were greatly influenced by these cowboy images. A great deal of the morality of the time was taught through these films and their corny story lines. The biggest favorites were Roy Rogers and Gene Autry. They were quiet, unassuming men who could sing and fight. They had romantic interests but sex was not casual to them. They fought only as a last resort. They never started fights but always finished them. Their sidekicks were as famous as they were. Grouchy old Gabby Hayes in the Roy Rogers films and chubby Smiley Burnette in the Gene Autry movies were great favorites. Another favorite was Red Ryder. He described himself as a peaceable man but always managed to get pushed into a fight which he always won. He had a small Indian boy named "Little Beaver" as a sidekick. Little Beaver was actually a child actor named Robert Blake who later made motion pictures of his own and starred in the television drama as a New York City detective.

Great debates would take place as to who was the best cowboy. Some argued that it had to be Roy Rogers because every film listed him as "The King of the Cowboys." Anyone could see that his horse, Trigger was smarter than any other horse. Others claimed that Gene Autry was actually better and that his horse, Champion was as good as Trigger and did things that were just as smart. Since the majority of the opinions centered around Rogers and Autry, no one ever seemed willing to defend any other choice. If a brave soul actually preferred Red Ryder, he was reluctant to speak up for fear of being branded an idiot who knew nothing about cowboys. Since Roy Rogers was my favorite, I had nothing to worry about.

I don't actually know when it all ended. Like many things that change, it is difficult to identify the exact moment when cowboys fell from the pedestal and stopped being heroes. I think that much of the blame goes to a new method of mass media that was about to burst upon the scene called television. The medium eventually made audiences more sophisticated and the next group of young people saw the old cowboy movies as pretty corny. Many years later my own children would ask me, "How could you believe any of that?" "How could they fire so many shots if they were only using six-shooters?" "If the Lone Ranger was really a Texas Ranger, who was his boss?" "How does he get paid?" "How come when people get shot, they never bleed?" These were good questions which never surfaced in my less sophisticated youth. Eventually, even I began to see the old cowboy movies as corny and my old heroes began to disappear. But they had already done their job. They made us all Americans.

A new kind of western, the adult western, would emerge. The central figure would retain some of the characteristics of the old cowboys, but now his clothing was dirty and less colorful and he was not necessarily clean shaven. His horse also lacked the colorful saddle and was no

PITCHING TUNES

It was the early spring of 1950. My cousin Pat and I liked going to the Congress Theater in Saratoga Springs to see the double feature movie along with a short subject and a cartoon. It was also the last year that Saratoga Springs would have vaudeville shows. It took all day Saturday to see a complete show. When vaudeville was in town, only one movie was shown after the vaudeville acts which were lengthy. The entire thing only cost fifteen cents for kids under twelve. My cousin Pat stayed under twelve until he was thirteen and a half. So did I.

One day the vaudeville was featuring a special act. On display in the theater lobby were several publicity photographs showing a young man wearing a Brooklyn Dodgers uniform. There were three photographs showing him in various stages of throwing a baseball. The caption that appeared above the publicity photos read "Pitching Tunes." This young man was a relief picture for the Brooklyn Dodgers. Imagine! A real major leaguer who could sing!

The young man's voice was actually very good. He really could sing. Although he was Italian, he did not have the impact on the audience of a Frank Sinatra or Perry Como, but we found him quite entertaining. Between songs he would talk a little about the life of a major league pitcher. Some of our local girls decided to joke around during his act and put on the "screaming bobby soxer" routine that was famous in the Frank Sinatra audiences. Of course he know it was an act and went along with it, joking with the audience.

After the show, the young man came out to the lobby and signed autographs. Neither Pat nor I was an autograph collector so we did not ask for one. I am not sure if this young professional athlete was a rookie but he was certainly just getting started in baseball because no one had ever heard of him.

That was the last year of vaudeville in Saratoga Springs. There were no live shows the next summer. In October of 1951 a former Saratoga Springs vaudeville performer was brought in as a relief picture in a final playoff game between the Brooklyn Dodgers and the New York Giants. The second pitch he threw was to a batter named Bobby Thomson who promptly hit the ball into the left field seats of the Polo Grounds to win the pennant for the New York Giants.

The young pitcher was Ralph Branca, who made major league baseball history that day and would be forever remembered for that pitch and not for the fact that he once performed in vaudeville, pitching tunes.

THE RED SPRING

Saratoga Springs is famous for its natural flowing spring waters (thus the name Saratoga *Springs*) which have always attracted travelers who were convinced the waters had medicinal and/or therapeutic value. Much evidence exists that Native Americans were using the springs in this manner long before Europeans ever arrived.

There are actually over 300 springs (most have been capped) which produce water containing various amounts of minerals. Each spring seems to produce a different variety of water. New York State chemists have analyzed the waters and have found various quantities of minerals like magnesium, iron and salt. The city fathers built pavilions over several of them and the state provided signs describing the waters and displaying the names they chose for the springs. One of these was called the Red Spring, probably because the iron content in the water caused red streaks to form on the stone outlets.

Somehow, a rumor began to circulate that the water from the Red Spring was good for the skin. I don't know how it got started or if there was any truth in it. It is quite possible that someone had a skin condition which was cleared up by Red Spring water. The water could have had nothing to do with it. There were many rumors about healing powers attributed to the Saratoga mineral waters and people came from everywhere to take the mineral baths at Saratoga. President Franklin Roosevelt, a polio victim, was a patron of mineral bath therapy and a great supporter of the State Reservation which featured mineral baths. People have always made many claims for the powers of the waters. I do know that I could never find any *official* reference making any claim for its powers.

The Red Spring rumor really caught the imagination of the older Jewish women who frequented the Kosher hotels, numerous in Saratoga Springs in those days. Remember, this was Saratoga Springs in the late 1940's and the Catskill mountain resorts, which would become known as the Borsch Circuit, had yet to be established. Most of the older couples who came to the hotels were immigrants from Germany and Eastern Europe and were probably familiar with spas. They would go to the State bath houses in droves seeking relief from various ailments and trying to prolong their youth. There were, of course, other nationalities as well but the Jewish women were the largest ethnic group by far. I believe the baths were the reason that the hotels located in Saratoga. Perhaps the facility reminded them of their homes in Europe. In any event, when they heard about the Red Spring, they descended upon it in great numbers.

It was a warm, sunny day. A group of us had been riding our bikes around the Catherine Street area and had stopped to play in the School Three yard. In the middle of the game, one of the neighborhood boys rode in and yelled, "There are ladies down at the Red Spring washing their tits!" After a momentary stare of disbelief, we stopped the game and every boy mounted his bike. It was not very far from School Three to the Red Spring and we made it in about two minutes. Sure enough, there stood a group of buxom ladies (probably all of them in their sixties) trying desperately to restore the beauty of their youth in the water of the Red Spring.
    The looks on the faces of the eleven and twelve year old boys who were witnessing this ritual would have made a great motion picture scene with this conversation: "That woman has the biggest pair of tits I ever saw," says one boy. "You never saw a pair of tits," says an older kid. After about five minutes of this bantering, it was time to leave. Back in the schoolyard, I got into quite a conversation with the Catherine Street kids about how things like this happen in

Brooklyn all the time. They refused to believe that I had seen boys our age urinate in the streets on a daily basis and that many women sat in front of their apartment houses on a hot summer day, all but exposing their breasts to the sun.

As I look back I realize that the behavior that was acceptable in Brooklyn was seen as abnormal in Saratoga Springs. Most of the women we had been watching were probably barely able to flee Europe with their lives and wound up in New York City. Many came from crowded small villages in Middle Eastern Europe which had probably not changed very much since the Middle Ages. Sanitary facilities were primitive by our standards and summer seasons were very short. One had to take advantage of the sunlight when it was available. Transplanting people from Eastern Europe to Brooklyn did not change their behavior overnight.

The Saratoga Springs of the 1940's was a different time and place. I realize now how sheltered kids were. They had grown up in a small town and had not been exposed to people who were much different from themselves. There was no TV or internet to bring the world to them. "Pornography" in those days consisted of photographs of nude pygmies published in the National Geographic magazine.

By the way, some of those women were also washing their faces and arms in the water.

HARD TIMES

The early 1950's saw Saratoga Springs begin to decline. Actually it had already started. In 1946 a Saratoga landmark, the United States Hotel, was torn down. The passenger train traffic which brought people in great numbers right across the street from the hotel's back entrance was steadily declining. More people were opting for the "motel" and motor inns that were growing in number. Most of the large hotels were located in downtown areas and were never designed to accommodate the automobiles that people were falling in love with. The war years also left the structure with a long list of badly needed repairs. Modernization would also be needed and the owners were not earning enough money to justify fixing or updating.

It was both fascinating and sad to see the United States Hotel, a beautiful structure torn down. We were fascinated by the wrecking ball that tore so quickly into the building but saddened when we walked home from school one day to find a block long empty lot. Although no one actually expressed it, we could feel the presence of that empty space. We did not know it would stay virtually empty for many years.

Casino gambling was still an open secret during the Saratoga summers and things were still very lively. We could all still hustle a buck or two by selling papers, delivering handbills, shining shoes and generally doing odd jobs. Everyone was getting along somehow with the summer season giving them a little extra.

Then, in 1950 the Senate Committee on Organized Crime was formed (a.k.a. the Kefaufer Committee.) By 1951, the gambling in Saratoga Springs came to an end. I remember reading about Myer Lansky being in town and getting arrested. He spent three days in the Saratoga County jail. All the gambling casinos closed. Even the poker games in the back room where I had once cleaned tables were shut down. Several gambling casinos in the Saratoga Lake area closed. The State of New York even tried to shut down the racetrack and move Saratoga's exclusive racing days to New York City. This would have happened if it were not for the people who owned the horses who threatened not to bring their animals to New York if the Saratoga Track was closed. We were lucky. Losing the track would have closed Saratoga down completely. For as long as I could remember, people in Saratoga Springs would rent their houses to horse owners for the month of August and use the money to pay their property taxes. It was bad enough with the gambling gone, but if the track had gone, the town would have ended up looking like any other city in the country that had lost its main industry.

In 1951, six years after the United States Hotel fell to the wrecking ball, the largest and most famous hotel met a similar fate. The Grand Union Hotel, long a symbol of Saratoga Springs prosperity and elegance was razed. Just before the wrecking crew got there, I took a walk on the great front porch of the Grand Union Hotel. The structure occupied an entire city block The front porch was very wide and extended the entire length of the block which fronted on Broadway between Washington and Congress Street. While I was walking down the length of the porch, I looked for the last time upon a floor made from white Vermont marble. This much marble would be worth a fortune today. I realized it would never be replaced. It was like taking the marble facing from the Roman Colosseum or the bronze from Hadrian's Parthenon. No one would ever build it again.

Eventually I came to the middle of the block where the main entrance to the hotel was located. I looked inside and saw that grand staircase, long a symbol of the hotel and once featured in the motion pictures "Saratoga Trunk" and "Saratoga." I would be seeing it for the last time. I noticed all the store fronts which had been built to open to the street side were empty. I stared at them and thought about how they had looked during the Christmas season when the merchants decorated them with multicolored lights. I gazed into the empty windows and imagined the Christmas trees spreading their arms over toys that no one could afford. The empty windows stared back and seemed to be looking for several small boys and girls, all bundled up and shivering with the cold, peering into them to see the beautiful and colorful things the window had to offer. I walked on.

In a short time it was all gone. A huge hole was cut in the fabric that was Saratoga Springs. The old hotel had covered an entire city block. The only thing left standing on that vast remaining space was a gray stone Episcopal Church which had occupied one lot on the Washington Avenue side. The hotel had been built right around it. It was the first time in many years that the Broadway side of that church had seen the light of day. It would be that way for a long time.

Not only was Saratoga Springs falling upon hard times but my personal life would also take a hard turn. My Father had been working at the International Paper Company in Corinth which was located a few miles north of Saratoga Springs. The road to Corinth was a two lane, winding affair. It tended to be treacherous at certain times of the year.

It was March 18, 1951. Dad was working the night shift. He was on his way back to Saratoga Springs early in the morning. His car went off the road and hit a low stone wall. These were the days before Ralph Nader exposed how unsafe automobiles were. Nineteen fifty-one autos were not equipped with seat belts, collapsible steering wheels and air bags. The impact caused Dad to hit his chest against the steering wheel which broke under the impact. He was a very tough guy and managed to walk away from the accident. Hitching a ride into town, he checked into the Saratoga Springs Hospital where he was examined and released. His ride took him to the Saratoga Eagle's Club where another friend was about to take him home. He collapsed and fell to the floor. An ambulance was called. Their efforts to revive him were in vain and he was DOA when the ambulance reached the hospital. He was forty-one years old. I was fifteen.

The event plunged my Mother and me into hard times. All we had was a two thousand-dollar life insurance policy. The policy had a double indemnity clause which would have made it worth four thousand in the event of an accidental death; however, the doctor who performed the autopsy reported that the cause of death was a coronary thrombosis (blood clot in the heart) and claimed the death was from natural causes. Consequently, the insurance company got out of the double indemnity. I estimate that the doctor probably got something like a five hundred-dollar bonus and therefore saved the insurance company fifteen hundred for his cause of death decision. All the medical people I have talked to about this told me that the blood clot was almost certainly a result of the accident.

This man who called himself a doctor took advantage of the fact that we were too ignorant to know that the blood clot was caused by the accident. We looked upon doctors as if they were gods. I know now that if we had challenged this cause of death decision, the insurance company would probably have given in. As I grew older and learned more about these things, I vowed that I would never remain ignorant or trust people simply because they are educated. I learned a valuable lesson.   Two thousand dollars was more money in those days than it is now but then it barely paid for the funeral expenses and the equipment we needed to open a dry cleaning and tailoring shop which we operated to support ourselves.

All this happened when I was about to enter high school. Up until then I was able to spend part of my summers in boy scout camp. The waterfront director was a young man named Tim Allen who picked me out as a candidate for the swim team. Excelling under his coaching, I became the lead swimmer. I swam breast stroke, free style and anchor on the relay team. We were not able to win every meet we were in but I personally never lost a race. The same was true for our relay team. I qualified as a lifeguard and was able to work summers at the Saratoga Spa Park when I was old enough.

My freshman English teacher, Miss Helen Doherty, encouraged me to write more and nurtured my creativity. She was the first one to really help me develop my language skills. At our 40th class reunion, I influenced our reunion committee to give a $1,000 posthumous scholarship to Saratoga Springs High School in Miss Doherty's name. She would have been very pleased that an English scholarship was given in her name. My classmates enthusiastically supported the idea. She was a great favorite who helped us develop as individuals. Not many people receive such an honor more than thirty years after their death. She was special.

I tried out for the football team. They had a policy that everyone who tried out made the team. I was injured in my first game and was out for the season. I found it very difficult to work in the dry cleaners where I had become an expert presser. It was exhausting to practice, play, come home to finish the pressing and then do my schoolwork. I recovered in time to try out for the wrestling team. I wrestled in my first year and was undefeated; however, having to split the time between sports and work was taking a toll on me physically and mentally. The actual matches were held on Saturday, half of which were on the road, and Saturday was our busiest time in the store. I had no choice but to quit wrestling.

My coach was not very understanding. His lack of understanding of my need to work made me feel very bad. He was the kind of coach who could see nothing in life but sports. He never understood that putting food on the table was more important for me than playing games. He was not a bad man but was probably a person who never had to face such a basic need. Many years passed and at our 30th class reunion, he and I discussed the situation. I was now a teacher and he was long retired. Time had caused him to mellow considerably and he admitted that he had made a mistake in my case. My answer to him was that I had now been a teacher for more than twenty years and I had made plenty of my own mistakes. It was nice to come to an understanding with him after all that time. He passed away before our next class reunion.

Mom remarried when I was in my second year of high school. My stepfather worked in Albany and I spent one year in Albany High School. I was assigned to a place called "The Annex," which was really an old elementary school building being used to relieve the overcrowding in the regular high school. Half the Sophomore class was assigned to The Annex, probably the worst half. Albany kids were a lot tougher than the Saratoga kids, but my urban skills, which had followed me from Brooklyn, kept me out of trouble. I was probably assigned to The Annex because I entered in January of my Sophomore year. A great number of the boys whom I met in The Annex had been expelled from a nearby Catholic school called "VI," (Vincentian Institute.) Somehow, I managed to fuse with that group immediately and found myself protected.

I only remember one teacher, Mr. John O'Hagen who taught English. He picked out one of my essays and tried to talk me into becoming an English teacher. I did not think this was a realistic goal for me at that time because I didn't think I could afford to go to college. Mr. O'Hagen was very kind. The other teachers in The Annex were not the same kind of people as Mr. O'Hagen. They did not seem to have the interest in the development of young people as individuals. Mr. O'Hagen did. Sometimes I went to school only because I did not want to miss his class. His faith in me kept me sane for the rest of that year.

I joined the YMHA swim team and we swam an official meet meant to lead to an Olympic trial. I had the best time in the region for the breast stroke. I thought it was quite good until I saw the times posted by the members of several California swim clubs. My coach explained to our team that the California kids had been swimming and training under experts all their lives and probably started in the water before they could walk. No one in our region even came close to going to the next step.

There were good and bad things about my stepfather not being able to support us. The bad thing was that I had to continue working to keep us going. I took the largest paper route in the city of Albany, NY. I had to get up at five in the morning, deliver the papers and then go to school. Most of Friday night, Saturday and Sunday was devoted to collections. I made almost as much money as my stepfather and we were able to pay the rent and get along. The good thing was that when it became obvious this could no longer go on, we decided to move back to Saratoga and take back the dry cleaning and tailoring store which had become available.

In the middle of my Junior year, we moved back to Saratoga Springs. It was good to get back. Saratoga Springs High was a much easier place to be than Albany High. English was still my best subject, but I missed Mr. O'Hagen. The other English teachers were very good, but no one could ever live up to him or my first teacher, Miss Doherty.

I finally overcame my adversity to mathematics but still did only what I needed to pass. I loved all the sciences. I took a course in typing and did well. I decided to take a course in Business Law and excelled. My teacher, Mr. Webster Coons, influenced me very much. Later, I would emulate him and become a Business Education teacher. I owe him a great deal.

I did not have much of a social life in high school because I was working all the time.
I was a little ahead of my time being considered a cross between a maverick and a geek, a smart nonconformist. I was still able to date a lot of different girls. The one girl I liked turned me down when I asked her to go to a school dance. Years later, I found out she married one of the more popular guys in the school. When I saw her twenty-five years later, I was a successful teacher and author. Her husband was out of work and she was supporting him. To be honest, she was nowhere near as attractive as I had remembered her in high school. I was surprised when she asked me to dance. She told me that she wished that she had gone to that dance with me. Actually, I had gotten over the incident a long time ago and was just as glad that she had turned me down. I was no longer the insecure kid she had known in high school who was probably attracted to her because she represented something I could not have at the time. I didn't have the heart to tell her this. I suppose this was a revenge of sorts. One would think that this revenge would have been sweet, but it actually did nothing but leave me feeling sad. Revenge is an overrated commodity.

There was a great athlete in my school who was always very nice to me. He is a successful businessman today and a person whom I still admire very much. I remember being envious of his height and athletic ability. Thirty years later, we were sitting together having a few drinks and talking over old times. He told me that he always envied my ability to write. I am still having a difficult time getting it through my head that I could be anyone whom he could admire.

The high schools of the 1950's were totally different from the high schools of today. We never did anything really bad. By today's standards, people would laugh at the things we thought were bad. I talked my friend Neil into putting himself in a locker because he was skinny enough to fit in. We had a kid we called Gus who once spent his entire time in study hall biting pencils in half. Everyone kept slipping him pencils until he had a pile of broken pencils in front of him. My friend Dana said, "Let's slip him a mechanical pencil." (Dana's idea, my pencil.) It took Gus the remainder of the period but he finally chewed through it. When I tell my own children about these incidents, they laugh to think that we actually considered ourselves bad. Having these acts judged as "bad" behavior points out the innocence of the times. It would not be long before this innocence would disappear and schools would begin reflecting a society that was about to undergo drastic changes.

JOIN THE NAVY, SEE THE WORLD?

With my stepfather working and the store going again, things got a little better. I did all the pressing and worked in the store after school and on Saturdays. Business picked up during the Saratoga summer and I began thinking about my pending graduation from high school. I figured that I would be drafted and decided to join the Naval Reserve. This meant one night a week in the reserve center at Glens Falls, NY. There were about five of us from Saratoga in the unit and we could take turns driving.

That summer I went to Bainbridge, MD for basic training. The store was going better now and my Mother could hire a part time presser so I was not needed as much. After basic training, the unit was assigned to a training cruise to Nova Scotia. The training cruise was great. We left the Brooklyn Navy Yard, through Long Island Sound and the Cape Cod Canal anchoring in Cape Cod Bay at Provincetown harbor. I was on watch that night, and while looking at the beach through my binoculars I remember seeing a man driving up into his garage. I did not know I was looking at Truro beach and that 40 years later I would be vacationing there, sunning myself on the same beach looking at the ships anchoring in the harbor! The next morning we steamed North to Yarmouth, Nova Scotia where the people were very friendly and the countryside beautiful. On the way back, we went on maneuvers off Block Island, which was then the Atlantic firing range for gunnery practice. I loved being at sea in spite of how hard the work was. As fate would have it, I would never go to sea again.

ACTIVE DUTY

Active duty in the Navy was fairly uneventful for me. I was assigned to shore duty at a place called Green Cove Springs, Florida. The base was part of the Atlantic Reserve

Fleet, called the "mothball fleet" by the sailors. It was located on the St. John's River, about 17 miles south of Jacksonville. Most of the ships were smaller, shallow draft vessels that had been used in the Second World War and were being stored there. There were more than one thousand vessels in the command.

After my turn in the kitchen, I was assigned to deck work. Deck "apes," as navy men called them, spent most of their time chipping and painting. Someone looked in my service record and noticed that I had taken typing in high school. I was called in and was offered a job as a yeoman (an office worker) in the gunnery department. This sounded better than being a deck ape, so I accepted. Later, I realized that this was the first time that education helped me to advance in life. Just because I was able to type, I was instantly transformed from a deck ape to an office worker.

I began thinking more about my future. One night, while standing a mid watch, I came to realize what was happening. The mid watch, sometimes known as the graveyard watch, is from midnight to four in the morning. My watch consisted of standing guard duty on the end of the pier. Someone had to protect the rusting hulks of the ships in the Atlantic Reserve Fleet in case they were needed in another war. It was January and northern Florida can get very cold at that time of year. Sitting down or leaving your post was not allowed on guard duty and I was pacing up and down on the four feet of pier assigned to me trying to keep warm. At about two in the morning, a young ensign (obviously just out of college) who was the duty officer for that night, was making his rounds. After I saluted and gave my report that all was well in my sector, this young officer went back into the duty officer's heated shack on the other end of the pier, sat down and had a cup of coffee. Even though it was on the other end of the pier, I could see it clearly.

A mid watch gives a person a lot of time to think. I practically re-lived my life. Why hadn't I studied harder, worked harder, saved more, learned more, etc., etc., etc. Watching that young officer go back into the duty shack and drinking coffee while I was out on the end of the pier freezing and unable to sit down made me think about the difference between that officer and me. We were very close in age. We were probably of equal intelligence. Why was he sitting inside where it was warm drinking coffee while I was outside freezing and staring out at the water? There was only one real difference between us. He had an education, and I didn't. It didn't take me long to figure it out.

I was also greatly influenced by another incident at Green Cove Springs. I came down with a bad case of the flu and was sent to the base hospital. The facility was located right across the highway from the piers. It once housed a naval air station which had moved to Jacksonville some years before. There was a sailor in the bed next to mine who also had the flu. We began talking, trading stories about our travels and home towns. He had been in the Navy about three years and was working in food service. He was from Philadelphia, PA and had quit high school in his third year to join the Navy. I guess when people are together with not much to do they like to talk about themselves. I must have been a good listener, because this young man told me a story I would not forget.

After joining the Navy, he had been on sea duty in Korea. When he returned to the States, he had leave time coming and money to spend. He went home to Philly. He bought a new civilian suit and went to a bar where all his old friends gathered. Naturally, they were all glad to see him. He began buying them all drinks. When they asked him what he was doing, he told them he was working for the government. "I didn't tell them I was in the Navy, or nothing," he said. "I only told them I was working for the government." "I kept buying drinks and the women were falling all over me."

I recovered from the flu and returned to duty. I could not get this young man out of my mind. I know how hard he worked in food service, having taken my turn in the kitchen. He had spent all this time working so hard just so he could go back home and act like an important man. I began to realize what I had witnessed. A young man with no education and no prospects for the future, other than to continue in the Navy, had nevertheless found a way to be somebody. He could go home once a year and be king for a day. I decided that I would become somebody. I now had the Korean War G.I. Bill which would pay for me to go to college. I was ready. I wanted more than going home once a year to being king for a day. I wanted to be like that ensign who had a future.

After eleven months in Florida, I was transferred to Bayonne, NJ to work on the conversion of the USS Little Rock from a conventional to a guided missile cruiser. I was going back North. The South had been an experience for me. As I was flying home, I remembered the first time I had gone to Jacksonville. This was the segregated south of 1955. It was a shock for me to see a water fountain in the park with two spigots labeled "white" and "colored." The northern cities of 1955 had their own form of segregation. We tended to be separated along ethnic lines. The division in the South was along racial lines. I thought how silly all this was. Our military base was in the South but not segregated. The same people who accepted integration on the base, including the housing for noncommissioned officers and their families did not accept it in town. I don't think any of us had any idea of the drastic change that was about to take place.

In any event, I was back close to home. I was able to go home on weekends and spend time with my family and I was able to spend more time with my Grandmother Elia in Brooklyn. The Navy ran a boat from the base in Bayonne to the military base in Brooklyn before and after work. It was a

81

short bus ride from the Brooklyn base to my Grandmother's house on New Utrecht Avenue. I visited Grandma at least once a week. It was worth it just to get the food. Her flat was the center point of the family, and there was always some relative there with food, money or anything else she needed.

I realized I had forgotten what city life was like. I was sitting at the dining room table talking to some of my younger cousins, when I heard a noise so loud it drowned out the conversation. The New Utrecht Avenue elevated train ran right outside the window of Grandma's flat which was located on the second floor. The noise was coming from a train speeding by. Everyone stopped talking until the train passed (about seven seconds) and resumed their conversation immediately after. The noise was so loud it actually shook the glasses on the table. I was the only one who looked around. They said, "It's only the train going by. You get used to it. After a while you don't even notice it." I also remember the conversation. My younger cousins were remarking about the influx of the Puerto Ricans into New York City. They were polarized on the issue. Half were arguing that they should be given a chance. One of my cousins, who was taking the opposite view remarked, "They're all grease balls." My Grandmother was quick to jump into the conversation. "No callum that!" she shouted. "It's a no right!" I explained to my cousin that his Grandmother got excited because that's what she was called when she was young and could not speak English very well. He, of course, could not remember those days. It seems there were a lot of things I had forgotten about city life.

It was nice that I was able to spend some time with my Grandmother Elia. She would talk about living in the same town in Italy with my Grandmother Schwerin and coming to the United States when they were young girls. When Grandma Elia died the following year, I realized what a godsend being with her had been. This was a strong woman who had outlived seven of her thirteen children. She knew mostly poverty all of her life. She brought up her large family in a tenement house in New York's Little Italy surviving the great depression. She was the centerpiece of the Elia family and its pillar of strength. When the going got rough, everyone rallied around her. She could not have been prouder of the fact that her grandson standing before her in a Navy uniform, planning on going to college. When she died, a part of us died with her.

I was still in the Navy when I was accepted to Siena College in Loudonville, NY. Just before anyone was allowed to be discharged, they had to be subjected to an extensive Navy propaganda campaign. All the "short timers," as we referred to ourselves, were forced to sit in a class and listen to a chief tell us why we should stay in the Navy. During the class I could only think about standing the mid watch at the end of the pier and the young man I had been with in the hospital. They were unable to convince me. I had other plans.

The day of my discharge finally arrived. I checked out with the Marine guard at the gate of the Bayonne, NJ station and stood waiting for the bus to Jersey City. I was due to be in college the next day. I looked back at the Bayonne Navy Yard for the last time. I could see the old USS Mission Bay, a small aircraft carrier which had seen action in the Pacific during World War II and had served as our berthing ship. It had been my home for over a year. The dirty old Navy Yard, busy with sailors, Marines and civilian workers (yardbirds) looked familiar and comfortable.

I looked the other way, away from the gate, and I was suddenly gripped with fear. For the past two years I had an interesting job, a steady paycheck and three meals a day. I knew where I was supposed to be and exactly when I was supposed to be there. I had experienced the comfort of being regimented. Now as I looked out into the street and into an uncertain future, I was afraid. I thought about the family that was waiting for me and would be there to support me. The fear became bearable. The bus finally arrived and I glanced out the window and said my final goodbys as the base disappeared behind the Bayonne houses.

COLLEGE YEARS

I arrived on the Siena College campus the day after I left the Navy. I decided that I would take over and expand the family business and elected to study business administration. I really wanted to study English but I could not figure out what I would do with an English degree. As it turned out, I became a teacher and probably would have made a good English teacher. I minored in English, my best subject, and in Philosophy. By the time I decided to become a teacher it was too late to change my major and I earned a teaching degree in Business Education.

Lewis Elia - 1955

Serving at Green Cove Springs, Florida

ENTER THE TV

The brave new world of television was about to be loosed upon the world. It started off innocently enough. Like any new product, it was too costly for most people to have television in their homes. The first sets appeared in store windows that sold radios and phonographs. Large crowds gathered at the windows to see boxing matches. The first televised match I remember was the heavyweight championship fight between Joe Louis, the then current champion and Billy Cohn, the challenger. In Saratoga Springs, a huge crowd gathered on the corner of Spring Street and Broadway in front of Hazard's store to watch the fight through a magnifying glass which was placed in front of a ten inch black and white television screen. Joe Louis won.

The local restaurants cashed in on the new technology. People began giving up the storefronts and would fill up the restaurants on Friday nights to have dinner and watch the fights. "The Friday Night Fights" became the most popular show in town.

As with all technology, mass production brought the price of the sets down and we were able to get one. Many of the old radio shows moved to TV. It was surprising to see what some of the radio performers actually looked like. We were already familiar with some of them. We had seen all the cowboys in the movies. Some of the old radio performers had also been in the movies (like Jack Benny and Bob Hope) but some we knew from radio only in our imaginations. I will never forget how disappointed I was when I saw Sky King for the first time. He was nothing like I had imagined him and his plane was also much smaller than I pictured. Only his daughter, a pretty young blonde starlet, was a big improvement over her radio image.

New stars also began to emerge. Milton Berle (Uncle Miltie) became the most popular star on television. His comedy style fit the new medium perfectly. He actually revived vaudeville. Many of the acts that appeared on the Milton Berle's show (actually called the Texaco® Star Theater) had once performed at the old Congress Theater in Saratoga Springs a few years earlier. The only difference was that Berle got into most of the acts himself.

There was also a new hero appearing before the American public. Professional wrestling had found a new home. The outlandish costumes, huge muscles and acrobatic maneuvers of these new athletes were perfect for television. The most outlandish was Gorgeous George, who dyed his long hair platinum blonde and sported a weight lifter's build. The most popular was Mr. America, Gene Stanley who kept winning every week. Many people were convinced that the bouts were real and the professional wrestler, a new born hero.

The wrestlers fought to a script which was totally predictable. The guy who fought dirty would get the advantage at first by using dirty and illegal tactics. Just when it seemed that all was lost, the good guy, never resorting to dirty tactics, would make a spectacular comeback and win the match. Sometimes the dirty fighter would win, but that was just to keep it from becoming too predictable. If a bad guy won, there was always a rematch and the good guy would redeem himself.

I was surprised when I visited my Grandmother, now in her late seventies, to find she had a
television set. Her sister, my Great Aunt Angelina, had lost her husband and moved in with Grandma to share expenses. Aunt Angelina was older than Grandma and walked with a cane. I asked my Grandmother what her favorite program was.

"E Moosh," she answered.

Obviously this needed more explanation. I asked her to explain what kind of program that was.

"You know, he'sa got-a gun, and a friend-a Chester."

I finally got it. It was Marshall (E Moosh) Dillon in Gunsmoke. I could understand their generation liking the marshal. He was carved from the classic old cowboy mold complete with comic relief sidekick. His morality was easy to understand. I asked if there was anything else she liked.

"The rassal," she answered.

This one was easier. They liked the wrestling matches. As fate would have it, they were just about to come on. My Grandmother, patiently backed up by my Great Aunt, launched on an explanation of what I was about to see.

" I see-a this-a-guy fight-a before," she said. "He's a dirty son-a-ma-beech." "I no like-a him."

I gathered that much on the second sentence.

"The other guy's a gonna give-a to him a-good!" she predicted.

When the match started, I realized I had found the two best wrestling fans in the world. They could feel the pain when the good guy was taking his lumps shouting "Ahhh, Ahhh" every time a blow landed.

Grandma turned to me and said, "You wait! He's gonna give it to him," pointing to the good guy who was indeed ready to make the spectacular comeback. When this finally did happen, I realized that they were shouting.

"Give it to him;" "Get him;" "No let him get up," they cried as my Great Aunt waved her cane in the air. When the match was over and the good guy won, Grandma turned to me and said, "You see, I tol-la you he would get him." "Si, he got-a him," echoed Aunt Angelina.

I said, "Grandma, this is all fake."

From the looks on their faces I knew instantly that I had said the wrong thing.

"Oh no, he'sa really hit him," said Grandma. "Oh no, is-a no fake," said Aunt Angelina.

I realized that I was facing a situation that was similar to the time I told Grandma that her home made macaronies were not going to turn to Polenta. Even If I had brought up the fact that the wrestling promoters testified before a congressional committee that wrestling matches followed a script, they would never believe me. So what! They enjoyed it. They worked very hard all their lives. They seldom left their homes. These tough, self-reliant, savvy, independent women who had buried children, grown their own food and otherwise taken care of themselves were completely taken in by the show. It wasn't the worst thing. If they were getting that much pleasure out of it, why should I take it away from them. I didn't argue. After all, I used to believe in cowboys.

Early 1950's

Mom in front of our ten inch black & white TV set with magnifying glass (filled with water) giving it the appearance of a 12" picture tube. There were no fights over what to watch since there was only one channel.

It was during this time that my cousin Pat died. He was forty-two years old. Pat had heart trouble and had to be operated on. Bypass surgery was not a very advanced technique at that time and he died shortly after he had the operation. I sat there at the wake staring at him. I remembered us carrying out the drip pan from our Grandmother's ice box, sliding down Dilly Lynch's hill in the winter and shooting the BB gun at old tin cans. I could smell the corn silk we were trying to smoke and hear the horses breathing as we were riding the old trail. The flag over Pat's coffin made me think about the fact that Pat had served as a gunfire control technician on the battleship New Jersey during the Korean War. I remembered when we came home from the Navy, Pat started a business as I went off to college. While I was still in college, I stood Godfather to Pat's son, Michael. Now I hugged Michael and stared down at Pat. The memory of my Uncle Danny, my godfather, hugging me and looking down on my Father, his brother, rushed back into my mind. It was the same spot in the same funeral parlor. This time I had lost a brother. I could not fight back the tears. Like my Father, Pat was too young to die. I could hear Pat's voice echoing in the back of my mind: "Kick somebody in the ass and they'll leave you alone," he said. I could see him climbing to the top of the tree at South Bend and jumping into the river. I remember when he came home married (I was still in the Navy) and when his son Michael and daughter Kathy were born. I stared down at his body, now forever still, knowing we would never talk again. It was a tough death for me to deal with.

My Grandmother Scarano was in the nursing home when Pat died. Grandma didn't miss much and knew something happened when Pat didn't show up for his weekly visit. I visited shortly after that and for the first time saw that all the fight had gone out of her eyes. "I wish the God would-a take-a me," she said. It was the first time I had ever seen my Grandmother give up on anything. She buried two sons, a husband and now a grandchild. Everyone in her generation was gone, her house had been sold and she was too weak to walk. Grandma was like a rock to me. The strong, peasant woman who used to lift me on her shoulders and carry me upstairs, bank the coal fires at five o'clock in the morning, slaughter chickens and rabbits for food, grow and can almost everything she ate and sing me to sleep with an Italian lullaby, now had to be helped into a chair. She lived about two more years, the quality of her life gone. Finally, mercifully, the God did take her.

Pat Ginocchi - 1953

Serving aboard the Battleship New Jersey

A RENAISSANCE IN SARATOGA SPRINGS

After college, and still living in Saratoga Springs, I became a teacher in Schenectady, NY. Schenectady is not far from Saratoga Springs, and I commuted for five years before I moved there. The group that went to college together began meeting at the old Colonial Tavern on Broadway in Saratoga which looked out on an empty lot where the old Grand Union Hotel used to be. A developer had purchased the Broadway frontage and was building a strip mall which would contain a supermarket and drug store. This really upset old Saratogians who had grown up with the elegance of the Grand Union Hotel in that spot. The resident artist in our group was a Saratoga man named Ray Calkins who made a remark that I will never forget. Looking at the box shaped building that was replacing the old hotel he said, "They must have gone to the (brand deleted) Cheese Company to get the architect," a reference to the fact that the building and the cheese box had the same architect.

As the late sixties and early seventies arrived, Saratoga Springs witnessed a revival. "Out of towners" began to discover the beauty of the city. The city restored the Italian Gardens in the park and businesses began to fill up the main street again. Upscale shops and buildings began appearing on the main street. New buildings began to appear where the old hotels once stood. There were so many "new" Saratogians, the only way you could tell the old crowd from the new was the fact that only the natives could drink the mineral water. Saratoga grew and prospered as the world began to discover what a nice place it was. Even the Princess Elena Society became active again and the Feast of St. Michael was revived. By the eighties, the town became a real upscale community with people from everywhere building houses and opening businesses.

My wife and I decided to have lunch at a restored restaurant located just off Broadway. The building that housed the restaurant was an historic site and one of the first buildings in Saratoga Springs. When I was a boy it was used as a laundry, so I was anxious to see how it had been renovated. There were tables and booths being used to seat the patrons and we were placed in one of the booths. As soon as I sat down I felt a strange feeling in the small of my back. I looked carefully at the booths and said to my wife, "These benches are the old pews from St. Peter's Church." My wife stared at me for a moment and said, "How in the world could you know that?" I stared back and said, "Because I spent many hours sitting in them waiting to be confirmed. I know that feeling in the small of my back. These are the pews from St. Peter's Church." We checked with the waitress and I was right. St. Peter's Church had been completely renovated and the restaurant had purchased the rejected pews.

A TRIP TO ITALY

During the years I spent teaching, I had the chance to visit Italy. I never got to see my Grandmother's hometown. Santa Maria di Castellabate is well off the beaten path in Italy and there were no tours in those days that visited that area. I did get to Napoli and some of the surrounding areas, but no closer. One morning in Napoli, I got up early and decided to take a walk down to the famous Santa Lucia Harbor. It's a bustling place with a lot of vehicles, deliveries, people, U.S. Navy personnel and various other commercial enterprises. One of these local merchants was a man in his eighties wearing white tropical pants and shirt which resembled a hospital patient gown. Over his shoulder he was supporting a wide leather strap attached to a huge metal box. He put the metal box down in front of me and asked me, in Italian, if I wanted a shine. I indicated yes and he shined my shoes. When I asked how much he said, "Five hundred lira, signore." The smallest bill I had was two thousand lira. I handed it to him. He responded that he could not change it. Since my offer only amounted to about $1.50, I told him to keep it.

I never saw such an astonished look on anyone's face. He could not believe that he had earned that much for one shine. He asked me to confirm that he could keep the money and I assured him that it was alright. He put the money in his pocket and told me to put my shoe back up on the shoeshine box. After I obliged, he opened a special drawer on the side of the box and removed a red velvet cloth. He then proceeded to give me the deluxe version of his shoeshine.

I looked at this bent-over old, Italian man whose stiff fingers were giving me the best shoeshine in Italy. When he finished, he looked up at me with the twinkle of satisfaction in his eyes. I responded that it was a job well done and how much I had appreciated his efforts. He stood up and put his arms around me. "Bravi, signore," he said. He lifted up his heavy box and began to walk off into the morning crowd. As I saw him struggling, painfully walking off to find his next customer, I began to think of what I had just witnessed. A poor struggling old man who knew that two thousand lira was four times too much to get for a shoeshine and could not take the money without earning it. His way of doing this was to use a special cloth he had tucked away in a secret compartment which was probably reserved for his best customers. Measured in monetary terms, he was still poor. In terms of dignity and self-esteem, he was one of the wealthiest men I had ever met. He was my Grandfather who paid cash for his house, bought a taxicab when he lost his job and tried to pay the doctor for delivering me before the doctor could get his gloves off. He was my Grandmother who took in washing, rented rooms in the summer and produced most of her own food. He was my Father who used his skill to build his son a swingset and my Mother who worked twelve hour days doing alterations to survive.

I had come full circle. I began to realize what the United States was and how my family had contributed to it. Italians, especially from the Campania region of Italy, were famous for their cooking. Italian food was so popular, it has become a great part of America. But there was a lot more to it than that. Not only did we put the garlic in the melting pot but we mixed our values in as well. The strength of our family life, the object of much admiration, made great contributions to our growth as individuals and to the strength of our United States.

I thought about all the different groups that came to America. Each had something to contribute. Every culture has a new way of thinking, a different way of looking at things. Every language spawns new ideas the exchange of which helps each of us grow as we continue to forge the American character.

How much we owe our ancestors. A wise man once remarked, "If the present generation stands tall, it's because they are standing on the shoulders of the last generation." No matter how much we accomplish, we must look down once in a while and see what we our standing on, and recall Cinque, the main character in the movie "Amistad" who talks abut his ancestors and reminds us that we are the reason that they existed.

EGGPLANT PARMIGIANA ALA GRANDMA SCARANO

It would be unthinkable to write a book about an Italian family without mentioning food. I am including a recipe for eggplant parmigiana which illustrates the resourcefulness of my Grandmother when it became necessary to deal with her new country.

When my grandparents, Antonio and Filomena Scarano, left the picturesque fishing village of Santa Maria di Castellabate in Italy's Salerno Province and came to America looking for a better life, they brought with them their cooking skills. One of Nonna's favorite recipes was eggplant parmigiana. Sometimes, however, the price of mozzarella cheese was beyond her means or not even available. My very observant Grandmother noticed that muenster cheese was sometimes lower in price so she tried it as a substitute. The result might sound sacrilegious to the "purist" of Italian cuisine but I can assure you it is spectacular. Later, my Grandparents settled in Saratoga Springs, NY (my Mother was about 4 or 5 years old at the time). Nonna Scarano passed on the "secret" of this dish to my Mother who taught my wife and me to make it.

Eggplant Parmigiana - Ala Grandma Scarano

Peel an eggplant and make 1/4" thick slices across.
Lay the slices out on a paper towel to get rid of the excess moisture.
Dip in egg and coat with seasoned, Italian bread crumbs.
(If you don't make your own bread crumbs, there are several commercial brands that will do very well - forgive me Nonna.)
Fry the coated slices in oil until golden brown.
Prepare the dish by spraying it with vegetable spray, then spread a small amount of sauce in the pan. To follow Nonna's recipe exactly, the next step would be to place the eggplant in the baking dish with the cheese slices separating them.

At this point my wife, a nurse, decided to change the recipe a little. She took the slices out of the pan and placed them on a tray lined with paper towels to let them drain before placing them in the baking dish. This resulted in less grease being retained and much healthier food. I must admit that I liked it much better. So did my Mother. I would be remiss if I did not give my English/Irish/Scottish Wife (who is an excellent Italian cook) credit where it is due. Imagine someone improving upon my Mother and Grandmother's recipe! Bravo, Linda.

Create layers by placing eggplant, muenster cheese, and sauce in the baking dish.
After the last layer has been placed in the pan, sprinkle generously with parmesan cheese.
Bake in the oven for about 45 - 60 minutes at 350 degrees. Do not over fill the pan; leave room for the bubbling of the sauce.
Left over portions make excellent sandwiches and they freeze well.

Nonna noticed that the muenster cheese had very good flavor and did not string like mozzarella. For years, everyone raved about her eggplant and wanted to know her secret. She never told anyone but my Mother (who passed it on to us.) We pass it on to you in her memory and as a tribute to her talents as a superb cook.